The
GOLF
SECRETS
of the
BIG-MONEY
PROS

JERRY HEARD

The
GOLF
SECRETS
of the
BIG-MONEY
PROS

by

Jerry Heard

with

Paul Dolman

Production Team

Project Director	David R. Yale
Lead Consultant	John Angus
Pro Consultant	Paul Dolman
Consultants	Michael F. McNulty, Gary Reed
Computer Consultant	Kevin McNaughton
Concept Development	Tony Fernandez
Creative Direction	John Angus, David R. Yale, Dan Zola
Editors	John Angus, Benjamin Suarez
Lead Graphic Designer	Robyn Bennington
Graphic Designers	Judy Boyles, Apryl Denihan, Nancy Giermann, Steve Haught, Ken Polcyn, Barb Sandy, Ann Wolf
Illustrators	Artists, Inc., Fred Boatman, Fred Browning, Bob Davis, Fox Art & Design, Larry Gianetti, Todd Moncrief, Dan Zola
Print Production	Tom Dube, Patrick Wenz
Quality Control	Betty Addessi
Photographers	Dave Baio, Brandon Hemphill
Proofreaders	Robyn Bennington, Chris Trumphour
Support Staff	Kimm Gotter, Sherri Peters
The Hanford Press	The Heard Golf Academy Home Course Campus Heard Golf Center Canton, OH 44767-0001 1-800-777-9876

*T*his book is dedicated to three very special people in my life ... To my Mother and Father, who sacrificed so much of themselves through the years so I could play this wonderful game ... And to Ralph Lomeli, who put in all the hours showing me the shots and making me practice, so I could play it well.

Contents

Foreword _____ by Johnny Miller

When I first heard that my buddy Jerry was working on a book called "GOLF SECRETS OF THE BIG-MONEY PROS," I said "Yeah, sure," and hung up the phone. When the phone rang again I became convinced it was true. Not that I didn't think Jerry could read or write (I'm joking, Jerry!) but, to be honest, I didn't think anyone could get him off the course long enough to actually talk and write about the game.

Jerry Heard is about the most determined, consistent and intelligent golfer I've ever seen. If he's putting his secrets in a book, then you ought to pay attention. Few of the pros I played with embraced the game as thoroughly as Jerry and it showed in his playing. I rarely saw him when he wasn't playing or getting ready to play the next day. He was and still is a student of the game, unafraid to keep learning the way he always did — by asking questions. He'll study anybody he thinks has something to offer and try to pick up pointers to improve his own game.

And that's one of the great things about golf — you're always learning. Jerry's won major tournaments all over the country, toured as a PGA pro for a decade and a half and will tell you that he's still picking up tips each time he plays. If a consummate player like Jerry can be like that, it's little wonder you're reading his book. And, if you practice what he's telling you, there's no doubt in my mind your game will improve.

I've known Jerry a long, long time. I first became aware of this hot shot somewhere around the age of eleven, just about the time he took up golf. We we were destined to be rivals, at least on the course. He was this whiz kid from central California and I was his counterpart in the northern California area. He was the best young player from the middle of the state and I was the best from the Bay area, so our paths had to eventually cross.

The first time we ever went head to head, Jerry Heard did what he's done to so many other players in his career. He beat me.

All I really knew about Jerry was his reputation, but then I saw him play and it was easy to see why this guy was going to be a force in the game. He was a lot bigger and stronger than I was — after all, he was a star high school football player — and he used that strength magnificently. He didn't just crunch the ball, he had a lot of muscle control and used the strength when he needed it and pulled it back for finesse shots. He's always had strong hands and strong shots; nothing hesitant about Jerry Heard.

At the same time, Jerry's always been a graceful player. Some of the tour guys with body strength tend to come on like weightlifters, but not Jerry. To be sure, he had a way of playing that used his strength but included beautiful knee action, smooth and self-assured putting strokes — none of the attributes usually associated with strong players.

Maybe above all else, he was a tough player. He hid it well by acting nonchalant, whistling and laughing in the middle of tournaments, but always hiding a mind that was calculating the next shot and never panicking when things got a little tough.

After our run-ins as junior players, we continued competing through college. I probably don't have to tell you that he was a great college player at Fresno State and every time we played it was a struggle. Jerry never lets up. It was during our college years that we became friends. Maybe our paths didn't cross often but we admired each other's style and once we were on the tour together, we discovered that our birthdays are only two days apart in the same year — his is May 1st and mine is April 29th. So, as he likes to remind me, I will always be an old guy compared to him.

Jerry and I have always helped each other fine-tune our games but there was a time in the mid 70's when he was faltering and I could tell his back was bothering him. After getting hit by lightning in 1975, it's a wonder he's playing at all! But I could tell he was hurting and because I've never had back problems, it was hard for me to relate to what he was going through. I could tell he just wasn't able to exert his swing enough. He was swinging so tentatively he either hooked it or blocked it off to the right and just wasn't able to control his drives the way he used to. I tried to help but it was like his mind knew what to do but his body just wasn't cooperating.

Jerry still doesn't hit the booming drives he used to. But this is where his talent and knowledge of the same really take over. Like I said, even though he's a big man, he no longer tries to kill the ball. Instead, he concentrates on course management, playing high percentage shots and using every advantage a particular hole can give him. I told you, he's a smart player.

One of Jerry's biggest influences on the tour was Lee Trevino. Lee taught Jerry, a natural hooker, how to fade the ball and really added a new dimension to Jerry's game. This happened around 1971 and if you look at the record of Jerry's PGA wins, you can tell that was a time when his game really took off. By learning from Lee how to play the ball just the opposite of the way he had all his life, now Jerry had both basic tee shots covered. If he faced a dogleg to the left, Jerry would use his old junior days swing and draw the ball to the left. If it was a dogleg to the right, he'd use some of that Trevino action and draw to the right. This was bad news for those of us who had to compete against Jerry Heard because now there wasn't a shot out there that scared him. Couple this with just an easy, easy swing to the greens and his accurate putting game and this guy was something.

I'm really looking forward to hitting the senior tour with Jerry. Because of the closeness of our birthdays, we'll be eligible about the same time and we'll go out together. It'll be just like old times. When we were on the tour we played all our practice rounds together and it'll feel good to be out there again, enjoying the game.

Jerry has a great philosophy that I really agree with. If anyone asks him why he's such a happy, friendly guy, he'll get a basic answer. Jerry believes we all have a choice. We can go through life angry and nasty or we can relax and enjoy the trip. Obviously, Jerry's a master at enjoying both life and the game of golf. But he's no pushover. I'm sure when we're on the tour again he'll be constantly reminding me that I'm older than him and it's starting to show. That's Jerry — always looking for the edge!

Keep reading and enjoy "THE GOLF SECRETS OF THE BIG-MONEY PROS!"

Johnny Miller

My Story

Let me tell you a little background on myself by starting with a few words of encouragement — if I could end up making a living at the game golf, then there's hope for everyone reading this that their game can be improved.

Most people have golf grow on them. You know, they start out slow, playing a little in high school or college, some more as they start their professional careers and realize it's a great game for social and business relationships and eventually they're playing the game all the time. I was a little different — the game of golf grew into me. I started playing seriously at a very young age and haven't stopped and never will.

I was born and raised in Visalia, California, one of the premiere farming areas of this country. My father grew peaches, oranges and grapes but he'd always been athletic and I guess it was just passed on to me. He played professional softball and took up golf when he was too old to run the bases anymore. It quickly became his main sport and a source of great pleasure.

My earliest memory of golf at the Heard household was the first time my father came back from a round of golf and told me he shot 110 to his partner's 96. I was really proud of him. I thought the highest score was the best like softball or baseball. There have been days on the course I've wished it were.

I was somewhat of a natural athlete, and played every sport I could through school. At eleven I started playing golf for real. And it's funny when I think about it now, but of all the sports I played, I was the lousiest at golf. But it didn't matter. I loved the challenge and I went crazy, golfing every single day at Sierra View, the local course. Early on it was probably the feeling of hitting the ball hard, as far as I could that was the most fun.

We didn't have a formal junior golf program or anything, so I was either golfing alone or with older, better players. Through watching and asking questions, I learned very fast and this experience was never lost on me, even on the tour. I always wanted to play with guys better than me so that I had to really work to stay up with them.

Well, it's the truth. By the age of twelve I was shooting par golf and beating nearly anybody who took me on. Even when I lost, I considered it a win because I always learned something and it would help me the next time I played.

From the very start, I took the game seriously and had my eyes set on being a touring pro. My mother and father gave me lots of support and it's impossible to overestimate the value of that.

Being a golfer, my dad took great pride in watching my game come together through lots of hard work. But he taught me to never forget that it's a game and the object is to have a good time doing it. In fact, every time I'd come home from playing, I remember my dad asking me one simple question …

"Did you have fun?"

As a kid growing up, Sam Snead was my hero and I did everything I could to emulate him. I tried to copy his style, used Sam Snead 100 balls, the whole bit. Everyone who succeeds has an idol in their chosen field and Sam was mine. I couldn't have known that there'd be a day when I'd not only meet him, but golf with him as well.

I kept golfing through high school and I think that was where I started getting my name around as a serious player. Just about every tournament I entered, I won and it didn't take long for the word to get around. It didn't hurt that I was a little loose and carefree — I think this attitude, coupled with my abilities, managed to psych out a lot of my competitors. After winning a string of junior tournaments, I won the California State Junior Championship and that really got my name around golf circles.

Eventually I attended Fresno State on a golf scholarship and continued my winning ways. It's pretty obvious that the more I won, the more it reinforced the fact that I was going to make my living as a professional player. Winning any golf tournament, regardless of the level of competition, is a tremendously satisfying experience. The higher the level, the bigger the thrill. When I started winning at the college level and in a hot bed of talent like California, I couldn't help but believe that I had what it takes to make a living playing this game.

I made money playing golf in college as well as winning tournaments. Hey, I had to. My father had ended his working career as night waterman at Sierra View — this was before courses had automatic irrigation systems — and he and my mother were far from independently wealthy.

So, to get extra money to help pay for school, I hustled games on courses around Fresno State. It's always easy to find someone who thinks he's a better golfer than he really is — part of this book deals with this problem of not seeing your flaws — and when they saw me, an apple-cheeked, smiling young kid straight off the farm, they saw me as a mark. But that perception was usually changed quite quickly once we started playing.

To be honest, I enjoyed playing for money much more than trophies. It always got my juices flowing that much harder to think in the back of my mind that a tough drive or tricky putt was the difference between being broke and having money in my pocket. This early exposure to "pressure golf" would pay off in big dividends as time went on. The more you experience it, the better you learn to accept it as routine.

While in college, I set a few course records and won more than my share of events. I was named Second Team NCAA All-American for both 1966 and 1967. I competed against the likes of Johnny Miller, Grier Jones and Hale Irwin.

After three years at Fresno State, I was anxious to test myself at the next level. So impatient, in fact, that I left school before completing my degree program. I would not recommend that for anyone else.

Before going on the tour, a golfer has to go through what we call "Tour School." This is a series of qualifying tournaments designed to weed out the "wannabes" from the "gottabes." These qualifying events are generally regarded as some of the toughest, most pressurized golf you can play. It's like Olympic trials or NFL playoff games. You have to compete for the chance to compete in the big show. I was fortunate enough to qualify and started my professional career at the age of twenty one.

To go on the tour, you need to have some money — it's just that simple. You need expenses for motels, food, travelling, miscellaneous stuff that comes up all the time. But, as a tour pro, you're pretty much working for yourself. There's no company behind you to take care of all the money out of pocket so, like a company selling stock, I found ten backers who gave me a total of $12,000; the idea being that they would get their money back plus a profit once I won a few tournaments.

Now, back in the 70's, $12,000 was a lot of money for a young kid to deal with, so I did what every responsible twenty year old would do — I spent it. Boy, did I have fun! One of the first things I did was outfit myself in some really sharp clothing. If I was going to be a pro, I had to dress like a pro, right? I bought shirts, slacks, sweaters, shoes. I was looking good. The next tournament I traveled to, every outfit I owned except the one I wore that day was stolen out of my car that night. You talk about bringing yourself back down to reality in a hurry.

So after a few minor bumps and bruises, my professional career started taking off and I was considered on the circuit as an "up and comer." Again I think the mental toughness of my early competitions helped a great deal. It was an exciting time, those

Jerry ... then.

... intensity off the tee.

... having a blast out of the sand.

... at the practice tee with Arnie.

... with fellow "young lions," Lanny Wadkins and Johnny Miller.

... "Country Roads."

... down the fairway with Lee.

Jerry ... today.

early days, and I learned a lot by simply staying quiet and watching. It would have been a mistake to start yakking up with pros like Palmer and Player and Nicklaus right from the start and I knew it. You have to build up a certain level of trust with these guys before they open up to you. You become friends, you gain acceptance and respect, and they feel comfortable sharing their experience and knowledge with you. It works the same way today but my mentors were Trevino, Snead, Palmer, and Nicklaus. Some of the best throughout the history of golf.

One practice round with one of these guys was worth a whole book of advice from your garden variety teaching pro. These guys had been all around the world, playing under some of the wildest conditions you could ever imagine; just being on the same course with them took my game to a new level.

The greatest thing you can know to improve your golf game is knowledge. If you lack knowledge you are not prepared. Knowing you are not prepared, you lack confidence. One secret I can share with you that every big-money tour pro will back up is: NEVER STOP LEARNING!

In 1971, my first really successful year as a touring pro, I made over $100,000 and was named Golf Digest's Most Improved Player. But thanks to my contract and the cut that went to my backers, my slice of that money was pretty slim. That's when I realized something had to be done. After some tough negotiations, I bought my contract back and started working for myself. I had $8,000 out of the $100,000 but I was free and my own boss again. In 1972 I made over $130,000 and was playing well. A highlight that year was my selection to the World Cup Team which would give me the chance to play on courses around the world. I also earned a spot on two Ryder Cup teams but certain rules in effect at that time prevented me from competing.

Funny how a guy will work hard on a career, building up a reputation and one little incident can put all that lopsided. Despite the years I've swung the club and the tournaments I've won, one certain afternoon I spent with Lee Trevino and Bobby Nichols some twenty years ago still stands out in everyone's mind.

It was 1975 and I was playing in the Western Open at the Butler National Country Club in Chicago. Over the previous years I'd won tournaments like the 1971 American Golf Classic, the 1972 Florida Citrus Open, the 1972 Colonial National Invitational and in 1974 I won the Florida Citrus Open for the second time. I was an established winner on tour and was a contender in major events. In short I was emerging as one of the best of the best players in the world.

Lee and I each saw the storm rolling in. Play was suspended and players and spectators were taking shelter as best they could. An official came by in a golf cart to take us to the clubhouse but with my left foot on the cart, Lee talked me into staying and riding out the storm there on the course.

We had heard that you ought to remove your shoes because golf spikes make you more conductive, so we sat down, shoes off, and started talking about who knows what. Lee was resting his back against his umbrella and I had mine held between my legs. When the bolt hit a nearby tree it made a deafening explosion. Apparently the current travelled through the ground, us and our umbrellas.

As we all know, lightning is really fast. Guess that's why they call it a "flash." For those few seconds during which I was actually being electrocuted, an eternity passed. Every muscle in my body flexed and convulsed. Both of my hands involuntarily drew up into fists and, for those brief few seconds, I couldn't open them.

I remember thinking at that moment, "I'll never play golf again!" I didn't think about my life or anything else ... only about golf.

I spent that night in the hospital with blood in my urine and an irregular heartbeat. Everything was a little out of whack, but they stabilized me and checked me out and amazingly I really didn't feel too worse for wear.

In fact, I stayed and completed the tournament, finished in the top 10 and made a nice check. But I should have known it wasn't going to be that easy.

A few months later my back really started hurting and when I talked to Lee, I learned he was going through the same thing. Lower back pain can really affect your golf game. It's surprising how many things you do everyday that are controlled by lower back muscles and are taken for granted. Many of you have or will have some back pain so you know what I'm talking about. The better shape you're in, the easier it is to come back from an injury and, for that matter, the less chance you'll get injured to begin with.

Our doctors laid out two choices — either extensive bed rest or surgery. Lee chose surgery and I took the bed rest route. Maybe I should have opted for surgery because although my back felt better after resting it never really felt right again and even to this day is sore from time to time.

I felt my confidence was shot and my game was slipping away and I had to make some changes. Adopting a less strenuous position at impact is a move I had to make to compete with the best players in the world. Learning to adjust and improvise according to your abilities and to play to your personal strengths is one the most important secrets in this book. I did and in 1978 was rewarded with a victory in the Atlanta Open. Ray Floyd is a wonderful example of this; his less than classic style has stood the test of time. He figured out the best way for him to play, perfected it and took it to the elite level.

After fifteen years as a top touring pro, I bowed out. I had a successful career playing the game and have enjoyed the last few years as Director of Golf at one of the finest resort destinations in the world, South Seas Plantation, Captiva Island, Florida. At the Jerry Heard Golf Academy we will teach players of all levels of skill and experience what I learned in fifteen years with my mentors.

What does the future hold for me? What else? The Senior Tour!

Although I have a few years left before I can qualify, I can't wait. Maybe it's warped, but I miss the daily grind of competing — the travelling and practicing, the competition and playing with the best players in the world.

The Senior Tour is a dream come true for the fans. They get to associate with the heroes of their youth, the golfers they looked up to when they were learning the game. And the older players seem to recognize and appreciate the support they've gotten from you, the fan, over the years. You could get along just fine without a Tour or Senior Tour but we certainly couldn't get along without you.

When I get back out there I expect to see you when I'm in your area. Let's have some fun together ... play a little golf, tell a few stories ...

Introduction

When the time came for me to sit down and write my book about "Golf" I thought a while about what type of book it should be.

And it didn't take long to come up with an answer.

If you go to the bookstore, you'll see that there are basically two kinds of books being written by pros like me ... the "Autobiography" and the "Instruction Manual."

Now I knew right away that a book about my life and achievements on the tour wasn't quite where it was at. Don't me get wrong ... as you've already read, I've been a very successful pro, and have led a pretty interesting life — and I don't have any problem telling people all about it. (In fact, once I get started about myself, some of my close friends don't have any problem politely suggesting that I try thinking about another subject).

But I don't want to tell you about my "life story" here. That's why I put all that up front and out of the way just so you'd get to know me better.

Because what I really want to do is tell you about the game of "Golf" — and give you the kind of solid, bottom-line information that will *improve your game*. And I'm not talking about general things that will make you feel better about the game and the way you play it ... I'm talking about *strokes*! Depending upon the kind of golfer you are now, I'm talking about knocking 4-17 strokes off your scorecard in a matter of weeks!

So if it isn't a rags to riches autobiography, it must be a "How To..." book full of mechanics and theories on how the swing really works. Enough books have already been written defining and explaining the golf swing. What the self-proclaimed gurus miss is that the golf "swing" is just one part of playing the game. This book will help you determine how you can learn to play your best game.

This isn't a book about "Jerry's" way to play golf. In fact, one of the things you'll discover is how important it is to find out how to play the game "your" way ... in a way that's most comfortable to you and how you're made up — both physically *and* mentally.

What *is* this book about? It's really very simple ... And, in a way, it's really not even coming from me ...

... It's the Golf Secrets of the Big-Money Pros!

I stepped back and took a look at my life on the tour. I took a look at the people I learned the game from firsthand ... the people I played with, week in and week out ... the people who became both my fiercest competitors, and my closest friends.

And I realized, these were "household" names in the game of Golf, at a time when the game was just beginning to blossom into the huge international pastime it is today.

I learned from the "legends." Guys like Snead, Palmer, Nicklaus, Casper, Trevino. My contemporaries were the "young lions" of their day ... Johnny Miller, Lanny Wadkins, and Grier Jones. In turn, we took what we learned from our mentors and what our own experiences taught us and passed it on to some chosen few out of the next generation ... Curtis Strange, Ben Crenshaw, Tom Kite, etc.

There's a funny thing about golf. Even though when you're playing good it's really a very simple game, there's always something you can do to make yourself a little bit better. Give yourself the "edge" you need to beat out those other guys who play this game for a living. When you're a "pro" you *have* to keep getting better to survive on tour. It's that simple.

And you know what I found out? Even though we're all out there competing against one another — putting our very livelihood on the line every day — we're *constantly* talking to one another about our game! If we're not bragging about what kind of shot we played to stick it two feet from the hole on "number 9," we're moaning out loud about why we couldn't seem to shake off the "voices" over that big-money putt on "16!"

It's just something golfers do. You know it. How many times do you finish your round and *not* sit around a table at the "19th hole" and talk it over? Well the pros do it too, and believe me, we do it as much like "pros" as any other part of the game.

But there's something else you have to know about all this. If you're not in the "community" — if you haven't paid your dues — these "secrets" are very hard, if not impossible, to come by.

I've paid my dues. And I've learned a lot of the "secrets of the big-money pros" along the way. It wasn't easy. And now I'm ready to tell them to you. This book is just the beginning.

In the Chapters ahead, I'll try to bring out these secrets in a simple, straightforward manner ...

- First, I'll talk about how important it is to get the right equipment. I'll tell you the secrets the pros know about getting the tools they need to get the job done, and more importantly, how you should choose the right equipment for yourself.

- Then I'll tell you about how to practice and prepare *yourself*. After all, your body is your most important tool of all. Are there secrets to getting physically prepared to play your best? You bet! And I'll tell you all about them in this chapter.

- Next is one of the aspects of the game I like the best — the mental part. And as you would expect, there are definite "psychological tricks" and "mind games" the big-money pros use to maintain the attitude and unbelievable levels of concentration they need to stay on top!

- Once you've gotten the tools, and put your mind and body in shape to play the game, it's essential that you know the golf course and how to manage your way through it for 18 holes. I'll tell you what you need to know before you tee off, and the secrets of the best golf "strategists" who have ever played the game.

- In the next chapters we're really getting down to business. I'll start by telling you the secrets of the "basics." You will learn the specific "keys" to playing the game — right from the mouths of those who made each particular part of the game their specialty.

- "The Seven Deadly Sins" is a snapshot of the very key elements the average golfer needs to conquer in order to start dropping those strokes. I've got a secret for overcoming each and every one of them!

- Now I'm ready to take you right down the hole — from tee to green! I'll tell you the secrets of Wood play ... Long Iron play ... Middle Iron play ... Short Iron play ... Chipping and Sand shots ... Putting. And remember, you will learn the techniques of some of the best players known for each of these individual phases of the game!

- I've also included a chapter on a part of the game that catches up to every one of us. We all get older. And when I think about what happened to me on that rainy day in Chicago, I want to make sure I recognize that when you play the game of golf, it's "in your blood." There are secrets to continuing to play the game — and play it well — even as you get on in years, or become physically incapable of maintaining your normal approach to it.

- And then there's a chapter titled "Secret Practice Drills of the Big-Money Pros" — though, I must admit, there really are no secrets to these drills amongst us pros, because the best ones are the ones we all use to hone our game. So now you can get in on them, too.

Finally, as I was compiling these "Secrets of the Big-Money Pros," I discovered a way of presenting you with two more very exciting tools to help your game ...

- First, there's "THE BASIC SWING CHECKLIST OF THE BIG-MONEY PROS" — that brings you through the dynamics of the golf swing, from start to finish. You'll dramatically see how each of 10 keys are singled out through 9 different parts of the swing.

- Then, after you've used this checklist to help put your swing together, it is followed up by "THE SITUATION CHECKLIST OF THE BIG-MONEY PROS" — a handy, comprehensive checklist of what to do for various types of shots, given particular situations and conditions that occur on the golf course.

Frankly, I believe that these checklists alone would be worth the price of the book if they were the only things you received!

And by the way, this book on "The Secrets of the Big-Money Pros" is only scratching the surface of what I plan for the future.

I've also got an exciting monthly newsletter in the works that will give you topical information of what's happening right now in the world of golfing technology, and more detailed information on each and every part of this great game of golf!

But that's all up the road. Right now, let's start finding out "how they do it!" Let's start uncovering those "Secrets of the Big-Money Pros!"

Part

The Secrets of Selecting the Proper Equipment

No matter what game you take up, no matter what field you're in, you need the proper tools in order to be successful.

Golf is no different.

Now I know that some people figure a club is a club, and a ball is a ball. While others think that if big-money pros use certain equipment then those are the tools that should work for them.

But let's face it, your intent is to shave strokes off *your* golf game. So the best place to start is in realizing that the biggest secret of all comes with buying that new set of clubs that will start you on your way ...

SECRET NO. 1: FIND THE CLUBS THAT WILL FIT YOU.

We've learned a lot about clubs during the last 10 years. Today, there's a far greater selection than ever before and you just can't fake your way through it anymore. If you're presently using the wrong clubs for the kind of game you play, you can lower your handicap merely by selecting the right ones.

I'm not telling you to run out and buy custom made clubs through your local pro shop either. There are many brands and types of clubs out there now that are readily available to the average golfer ... all in relatively the same price range.

And the point is that a certain type of club isn't particularly better for you simply because it costs more. There are specific grips, shafts, and clubheads designed for specific ways people play the game. So don't leave it up to chance. You need to know enough about your game, and your own preferences to make the *right* decision when you buy those clubs!

SECRET NO. 2: GET A COMFORTABLE GRIP.

A lot of people overlook the importance of getting the right "grip" on their golf club. But when you think about it, that's where you actually "interact" with the club itself. And to do it properly, the grip of the club has to allow you to get your hands in the proper position... (which I'll cover in detail later on).

If your hands are bigger than average, the grip of the club will have to be bigger in circumference to avoid "wrapping" your hands too much around the club. You can buy grips that will adjust for this.

There are also grips that have a built-in "reminder" ridge down the underside of the club. Some golfers may find this more — or less — comfortable than the simple standard "round" variety. It's up to you.

Larger grips tend to decrease hand action during the swing. Conversely, smaller grips

1

encourage hand action. Choose grips which fit your shot pattern.

Finally, there's the whole issue of "leather" grips vs. "rubber." Leather will cost you more, and it does give you the "tactile" feeling you need to hold the club loosely without it slipping in your hands even in wet weather. The latest soft rubber grips on the market are about as good nowadays and a lot cheaper. The rubber and cord combinations are good and last longer than some pure rubber grips but are pretty rough on your hands.

SECRET NO. 3: CONSIDER A GRAPHITE SHAFT.

With the introduction of graphite shafts, the whole issue of choosing the right shaft for your game has gotten a lot more complicated.

Used to be, there was only one kind of shaft when they played the game on the links of Scotland — a hickory stick. As time went on, we moved to steel shafts, and then lightweight steel.

Lightweight steel was followed briefly by "feather light" steel and then "graphite" came along and kind of revolutionized the industry. They introduced a new "feel" to the club. The earliest graphite was characterized by whippiness and a tendency to twist at impact. This resulted in sporadic shot patterns. Although they contributed to increased distance, they lacked the accuracy and reliability that better players demand.

There are now basically three major types of shafts to choose from — steel, graphite, and titanium. To tell you the truth, the distinctions between graphite and titanium are very small, and are probably more psychological and cosmetic than functional.

The point of the graphite/titanium materials over traditional steel is in the weight. The weight saved in new shafts can be used to add to the clubhead or to add to the overall length of the club without making the total weight of the club greater. With more 'useable' weight, you get a more productive club. With some manufacturers, you will actually end up with lighter clubs overall. This helps many players achieve greater clubhead speed over the traditional materials.

Of course, the more flexible the shaft, the more you will "feel" the drag of the clubhead as you swing. Though steel shafts can offer certain degrees of flexibility, it is nothing close to the options you can get with graphite. There are many different flexes, different flex points, and torquing qualities. These attributes have an influence on "feel" and shot patterns as well as distance and direction. Lower flex points tend to hit higher shots and higher flex points hit lower shots. "Low torque" shafts resist the club's tendency to twist upon impact. This may increase accuracy, but it will also affect "feel".

Now, I'm not suggesting that all of you run out and get a custom-made graphite shaft, scientifically adjusted to your particular swing ... but it can be done. In fact, that's something tour pros are really into. The point I'm making here is that you don't have to settle for just regular or stiff shafts anymore. Don't select your next set of clubs based solely upon what the pro or a salesman has on his shelf at that moment. Go on out and start swinging those graphite clubs in the golf shops. Experiment! Borrow clubs from your friends. You just might find one that really feels right!

SECRET NO. 4: MATCH THE CLUBHEAD TO YOUR GAME.

With all the brands of irons out there today, there are really two major categories that will help you determine the kind of clubhead that's right for you.

One is what you might call "conventional" irons. They're the ones that I grew up with. Pretty basic. If you hit it right on that sweet spot in the middle, you'll know it. Miss it by just a fraction of an inch and ... well, you'll know that too.

The other type is what we call "game improvement" clubs. By adding a little weight toward the parameter of the clubhead, they've been able to expand the size of that sweet spot. So the average golfer doesn't have to hit it dead solid perfect every time to get the same result. But they sacrifice a little bit at the same time. And this is where the real secret comes in.

If you're say, a 10 handicapper or over, the average guy who scores in the eighties or low nineties maybe, you'll want to have a game improvement club. It'll give you the results you're looking for as far as hitting a solid shot just about every time. And, believe me, your score will show it.

If you grew up on conventional clubs, it's hard to change. The game improvement clubs won't "talk back" to you like a conventional iron will. What I mean by that is, you won't know if your swing is that quarter of an inch off target that could be the difference between playing good golf and really great golf. The bigger sweet spot evens everything out. But, I think the playability of the newer clubs outweighs the shortcomings some people see.

The bottom line? Let today's technology work for you. Don't play a harder game than you have to out of an ego thing. More and more tour players are using game improvement clubs. Gather all the information you can and sort out the marketing hype from the facts.

SECRET NO. 5: CONSIDER "METAL" WOODS.

So far, I've kind of been talking about irons. (Though you also have your "game improvement" and "conventional" woods as well). Now I'd like to cover one of the latest "controversies" in golf's more recent technology ... the metal wood.

Everybody asks me, "Why a metal wood?" Well I'll tell you why. Because it'll improve your game.

There's a reason why you're seeing more and more of them on the tour. They're lighter, more consistent, and easier to hit off the fairway than "wood" woods. Tight lies, wet fairways... put the wooden clubs away.

The two basic types of "wood" woods are those made from one solid "block" (usually persimmon) and those that are "laminated." Actually, while the solid block is more on the high price end of the scale, the laminated varieties are probably more consistently constructed, as far as what is available to the general public. Laminates are usually cheaper than solid persimmon too. Another important fact to consider is that the "insert" is the only part of the wood that contacts the ball anyway. So what you probably have is a "plastic" rather than a "wood".

That's another reason to seriously consider a metal wood. They're more consistently constructed, and you can get your hands on a lot of varieties to match your game.

SECRET NO. 6: START USING A "LOFTED" WOOD.

What I'm really talking about here is the "5 wood," though there are also "6's," "7's," and up that fit into the same general category.

If you've been playing for a while, when you bought your first set of clubs you probably got the Driver, and then maybe a 3 and a 4 wood. The average golfer isn't quite sure about the ins and outs of playing a 5 wood. I'll tell you more about how to play it later, but what you should know is this ...

A 5 wood is easier to hit than a 1 or 2 iron. So what you do today is take one of those irons out of your bag and replace it with a 5 wood. Or, try another more lofted wood if it fits your game better. You'll get a higher, more lofted shot, and you'll get the same distance as with those irons.

A 1 iron has approximately the same loft as a 3 wood, a 2 iron is about the same as a 4 wood and a 3 iron pretty much equals a 5 wood.

You know what they say, "Only God can hit a 1 iron" ... but, God, can you *ever* hit a 5 wood!

SECRET NO. 7: CONSIDER USING 3 WEDGES.

An added bonus of replacing a few irons with a 5 wood is that you've made room in your bag for an extra club.

You may have heard that Tom Kite was the first to use three wedges on the tour. Now we all do. And though you might think it's getting kind of carried away with the short game, it really makes a lot of sense.

First, you can never, EVER pay too much attention to the short game. There are so many situations that come up, you simply have to be prepared to play any shot imaginable. And, you have the right club in your bag to do it. Here's what the three wedges are for ...

First, there's the Pitching Wedge. It's got a lot of loft (about 50 degrees). And it's great for getting the ball up in the air around the green. That's what it was designed for.

Then there's the Sand Wedge. Even more loft, (about 55 degrees) which is great. We can always use a club with a little more loft to give us a little more lift in touchy situations. But a Sand Wedge was designed for getting out of a bunker. There's a built-in flange that sticks out underneath to keep you from burying the club in the sand when you're trying to "blast" the ball out. Trouble is, when we try using that club around the green, it can "bounce" off of hard ground so it's harder to get under the ball.

So on tour we all started customizing our sand wedges by grinding that flange down flatter. And all of a sudden, "Hey, we've invented a new club!" Now, the manufacturers are making a variety of wedges in many choices of loft, bounce and flange designs. Experiment with these clubs and choose the ones that fit your game and your golf course. Remember, you can *never* pay too much attention to your short game.

SECRET NO. 8: CONSIDER A HEEL AND TOE WEIGHTED PUTTER.

Just a short thing about putters. The way I see it, a putter is a very personal thing. Nobody should try to tell someone else that one particular putter is better than any other. You've just got to go with what feels right for you.

But just to give you some guidance, there are a few categories of putters ... There's the "blade," such as the Palmer Original, Wilson 8802, Tommy Armour Iron Master and others. There are "mallet heads" such as the Zebra or the Otte Chrisman. There are "heel shafted" putters and "center shafted" putters as well as "goosenecks" and "offsets." There are about as many *styles* as there are people playing the game. One man's gimmick is another man's answer.

One design feature with proven merit though, is the "heel and toe" weighted putter (e.g. Ping, Taylor Made, Inertial, etc.) As will be discussed in more detail in a later chapter, hitting putts solidly on the "sweet spot" is paramount to consistent putting, the larger sweet spot swings the odds in your favor. Nothing in putting is more important than feel, but if you can acquire good feel with a heel and toe weighted putter, I think you'll putt more consistently than with an old style putter.

SECRET NO. 9: CHOOSE A BALL TO MATCH YOUR GAME.

Finally, a word about balls. The secret here is, again, find the one that matches the way you play and the conditions on your course. There are two major considerations in selecting the right ball for you. First is the cover material and second is the inner construction of the ball.

Ball choice is kind of a series of compromises. The harder covers are more resistant to cuts and abrasions. The softer covers cut easier but because you can spin them more easily, they offer more control.

1

The cores consisting of a center and windings add to the spin rate of a ball, however, as a general rule, the solid core brands fly farthest. I think it's harder to work the solid ball and my experience is that I don't have as good of distance control with them.

Experiment to see what fits your game and your normal course conditions best. Some brands are definitely better than others, particularly when it comes to consistency. Also, many companies making hard cover, solid balls are beginning to make softer cover, solid balls. I've used some of these and certain brands are really pretty good. Even today's tour players are beginning to use them.

The most inconsistent type of ball in my experience has been the wound ball with the harder cover.

As a final note here, if you spin the ball left or right quite a bit (hook or slice), you probably ought to stay away from the higher spinning balls.

FIND THE CLUBS
THAT WILL FIT YOU

There are many brands and types of clubs out there now with specific grips, shafts, clubheads, etc. Finding the right combination for your level of play could make a big difference. You need to know enough about your own game to make the right buying decision.

SECRET No. 2

GET A COMFORTABLE GRIP

A lot of people overlook the importance of getting the right "grip" on their club. The most important things to consider are getting the one that fits your hand size, and that you get your clubs re-gripped regularly.

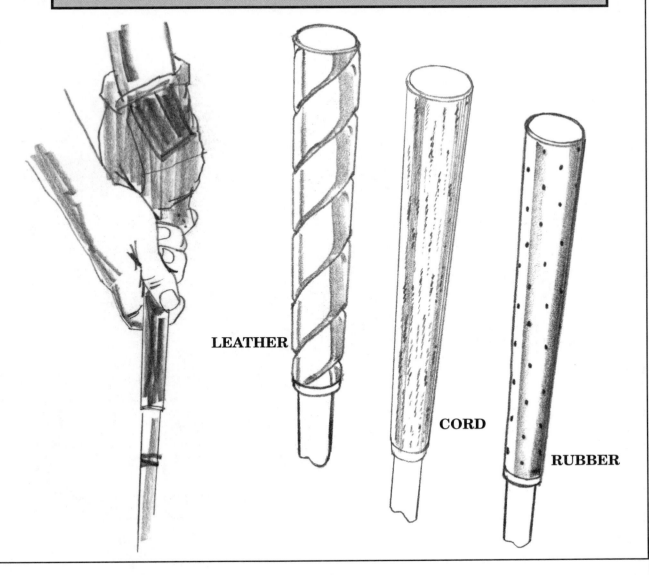

LEATHER

CORD

RUBBER

SECRET No. 3

CONSIDER A GRAPHITE SHAFT

There are many different types of shafts on the market today. While most steel shafts offer a certain degree of customization, they don't come close to the options you can get with graphite. If you invest in a graphite shaft, be sure to test several types, flexes, and brands to be sure you get the right one for you.

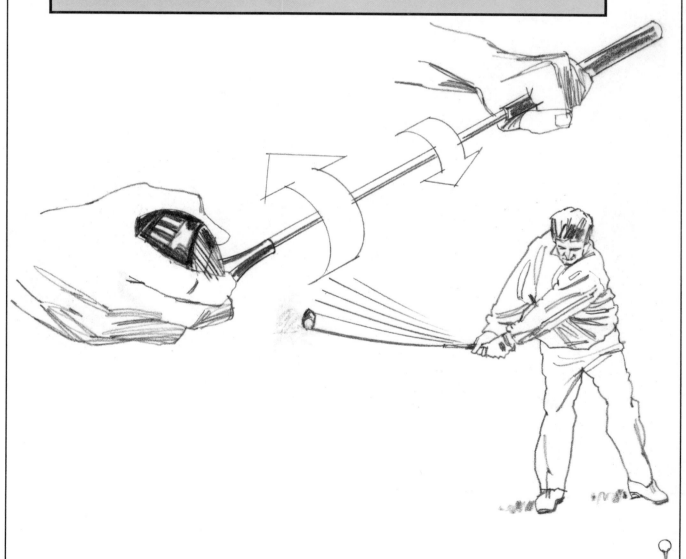

SECRET No. 4

MATCH THE CLUBHEAD
TO YOUR GAME

Today's "game improvement" clubs can help players at all levels of ability. If you're still using conventional irons out of sentimental attachment, make a nice display for them in your den and get in on today's technology with some new clubs.

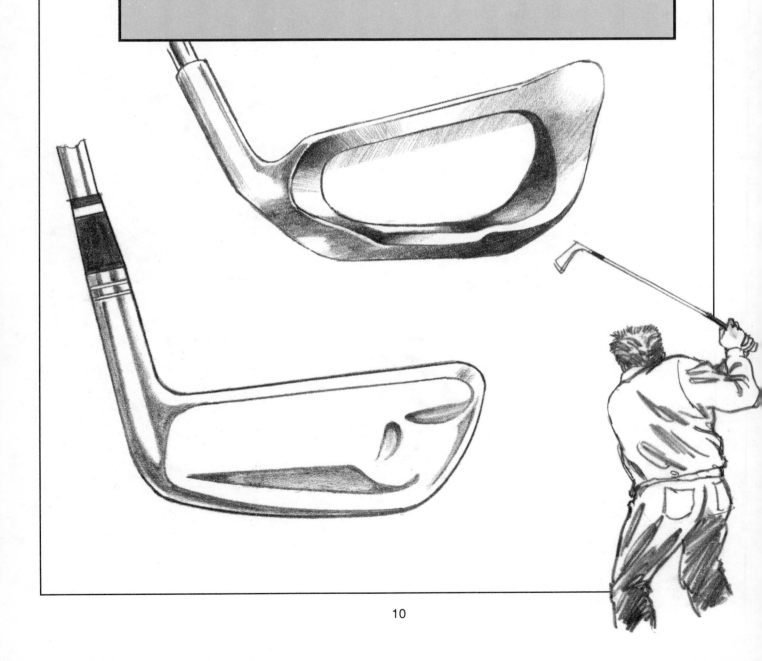

CONSIDER "METAL" WOODS

There's a reason why you're seeing more and more metal woods on the tour. They're more forgiving on mishits, more consistently constructed, and are easier to hit off the fairway than "wood" woods. There are also many more varieties available to match your game.

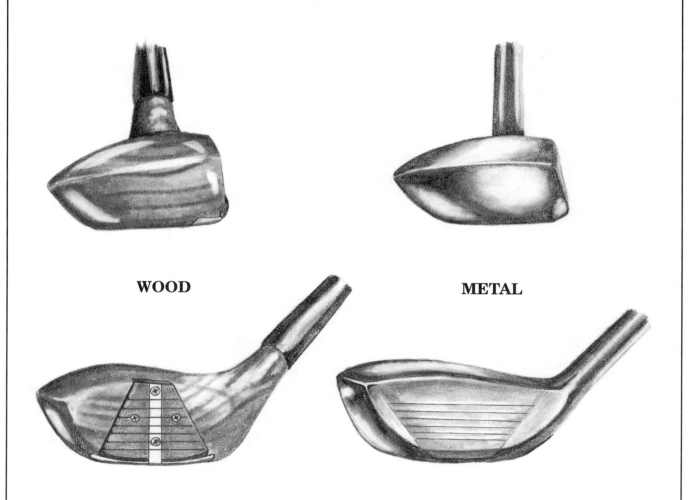

WOOD   METAL

SECRET No. 6

START USING A "LOFTED" WOOD

Most average golfers probably didn't get a "5 wood" with their first set of clubs. You should get one — or even a 6 or 7 wood — to replace your 1 and 2 irons. They are easier to hit, especially out of the rough, and give you a higher shot.

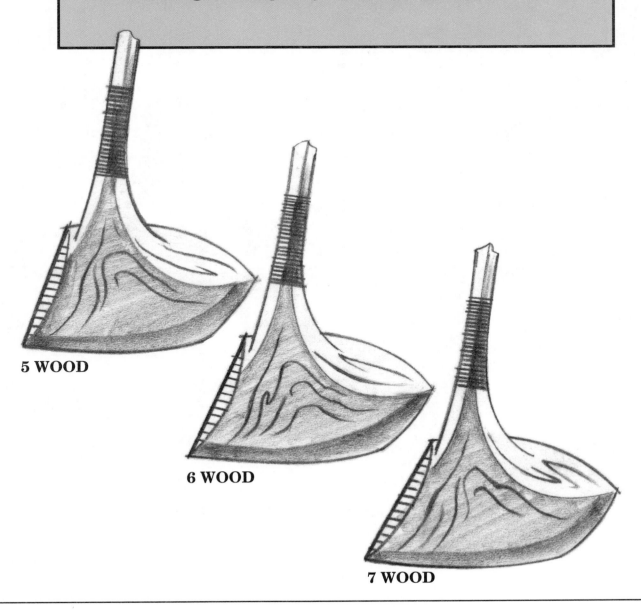

5 WOOD

6 WOOD

7 WOOD

CONSIDER USING 3 WEDGES

A lot more of the pros are using three wedges on tour. The Pitching Wedge has about 50° of loft. The Sand Wedge gives you even more — but yours probably has a large flange underneath to keep the club from cutting too deeply into the sand. A third wedge could have as much as 60° of loft or less bounce out of the flange or some combination of both.

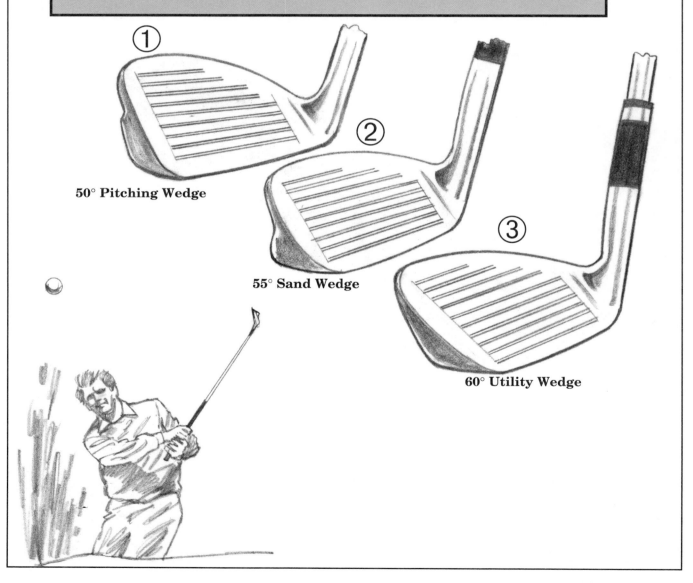

① 50° Pitching Wedge

② 55° Sand Wedge

③ 60° Utility Wedge

SECRET No. 8

CONSIDER A HEEL AND TOE WEIGHTED PUTTER

A putter is a very personal thing. There are many styles available. Choose the one that is most comfortable to you. But be aware of the ones on the market today that distribute the weight on the heel and the toe, and offer a larger "sweet spot." If you can get the "feel" of these putters, they could improve your game.

CHOOSE A BALL
TO MATCH YOUR GAME

Two considerations: 1) Balls with balata covers and wound centers will give you more spin and control, but will cut more easily if you don't hit them well. 2) Solid balls with harder covers may cost you some control but, as a rule, will fly the farthest.

Part

The Secrets of Practice & Physical Preparation

Now that you've got the right equipment, or at least are on your way toward selecting the tools that will do the best job for you, it's time to concentrate on getting your game and your body in shape to play your best.

Like anything else, to become a better player you need to practice. It's *so* important. Entire books have been written on this one subject alone. I won't try and go over every single practice technique or drill here, but I will give you the major scoop on practicing from a pro's perspective.

Prior to practicing or playing, however, you will benefit greatly from a good, but single, warm-up routine.

SECRET NO. 10: ESTABLISH A WARM-UP ROUTINE.

Getting comfortable with a regular warm-up routine is all a part of getting your body and mind ready for the round ahead.

On a day when I'm playing, I usually sleep as late as I can, stretch, relax a little, don't exert myself, and head off to the golf course.

My warm-up routine usually consists of swinging a weighted club or "donut" for a couple of minutes, then starting out with some half wedge shots to a target maybe 75 yards away. Then I work up to a full swing and skip my way through the bag from wedge to 8 iron, 5 iron, 3 iron. I will hit maybe five or six balls with each club and I will aim each shot at or over a specific target. I sometimes hit a couple or three fairway wood shots and no more than three or four drivers. You don't want to wear yourself out.

Some guys like to hit a few chip shots, but I never made that part of my routine. Spend ten or fifteen minutes on the practice green just before going to the first tee to get a feel for the speed of the greens and to reinforce your short putt mechanics. Don't spend too much time putting though. You don't want your back to tighten up on you.

I don't eat breakfast on tournament days because I like to be a little hungry when I start out on the course. Midway through the round I like to have a nutritious snack. Most pros do. Usually I have fruit — an orange or an apple — or an energy bar. Otherwise, I'd start running out of juice around the 14th or 15th hole.

I don't necessarily recommend this particular routine for everyone. But it works for me. You should do whatever works for you. Some pros have such a strict routine that they eat the same foods every night before they play and, in some cases, every night of the week. That may be carrying it a bit far, but it is important to watch your diet and eat properly.

Diet is so important. If you eat before you play, eat lightly and have a snack during the round. (Al Gieberger was especially noted for the peanut butter and jelly sandwiches he would carry around with him). I also stay away from coffee, tea, or colas before or during play. They don't help my nerves. A golfer wants to stay slow and calm with steady nerves, not uptight and jumpy. It's also good to know which weight you play best at and try to maintain it.

2

SECRET NO. 11: COMMIT TO PRACTICE.

As I'll cover later on, golf is very much a "mental" game. Real success comes when you have the confidence in your ability to go out there and just "let it happen." You have to know — without a doubt — that your swing is just the way you want it. Then you can concentrate on the strategic part of the shot, set yourself up in the proper position, and then just pull the trigger.

The only way to get to this level of confidence is through hard work. As with anything else in life, don't expect to get more or less out of your game than you are willing to put into it in practice. Depending on your commitment toward improving, try to settle on a regular practice schedule. Plan on doing it at specific times so it's not so easily forgotten or put on the back burner. The golf swing is a motor skill, like learning to drive a standard transmission car. Through repetition our muscle reaction becomes smooth and almost thoughtless.

Your swing mechanics should be practiced with a 6 or 7 iron, for two reasons. First, they are easier to control, so you won't worry so much about ball flight while you should be concentrating on mechanics. Secondly, you can hit a lot more balls with these clubs than you can with a driver before you're tired and beyond learning.

The more of the mechanics you can perform without thinking, the more automatic and consistent your game will become. Groove it, practice it, repeat it over and over. Yes, as nearly perfectly as you can, but even if your natural swing isn't very pretty, if you can repeat it and count on it to be the same time after time, you are going to be able to play good golf.

SECRET NO. 12: AIM IT.

Too often I see the average golfer go out to the driving range, pull out the driver, and start whacking the big ones.

First, warm up by stretching. Swing two or three clubs at a time or a weighted club. When you're loose, start with a short iron like a wedge or 9 iron, pick a target and start hitting 3/4 shots. Build up to your full swing but always hit your practice shots toward a specific target.

In keeping with always having a target, there is almost nothing more important than practicing good alignment. One of the principal weaknesses in the average player's game is his inconsistency in alignment, set up, and ball position. It would be a good idea to build a practice position for yourself by using clubs on the ground, biodegradable paint, etc. Since your alignment and pre-shot position has more to do with the result of a given shot than your actual swing does, it makes a lot of sense to work hard on it. One last piece of advice regarding alignment — if you're not perfectly square to your target line, be a little open to it. If your stance is a little closed (which many average golfer's stance is) your left side will cut off your follow through and will contribute to a poor swing. Being a little open actually helps clear the left hip a little.

Lastly, when you're swinging well and playing well, don't overdo the practice. I know there are alternative views on this but I learned early on from Lee Trevino. ..."If it ain't broke, don't fix it."

Practice the shots and situations that have been giving you the most trouble. Hit some shots from bad lies. Hit intentional draws and fades. Play shots while thinking of certain trouble spots for you on the course. Most weekend players don't practice the short game nearly enough. Work on chips, pitches and putts as much as you work on the rest of the clubs in your bag.

SECRET NO. 13: WHEN IT FEELS GOOD — STOP.

Speaking of confidence and positive feedback, always end a practice or warm-up session with a solid shot.

If you're near the end of your practice or warm up and you feel like you're really in the groove ... stop. If you only have five or 10 balls left, leave them on the tee, and walk away.

Sometimes we tend to overdo it while practicing. I don't like to go beyond a half-hour. Maybe 10 minutes putting, about 20 minutes on the range. That's about it. Practice too much and you not only use up energy, but it starts to feel too much like work. Remember, you're out there to groove your swing. Don't overdo it. When you see those good shots coming time after time, stop, and save them for the golf course.

SECRET NO. 14: GET ANOTHER PAIR OF "EYES."

A big thing about being a pro is that you have a tendency to get too far "into" yourself. It's so important to establish your own game that sometimes you go too far. You feel that you're doing something wrong, but you have no way of seeing it because you're "in" there ... trapped in the eye of the storm.

That's when you have to step back and get a fresh perspective. You need another pair of "eyes." And by that I mean you rely on other people to help get you back on track.

You need to talk to someone familiar with your swing, someone whose judgement you trust and someone you play with regularly. We do it all the time on the tour. In fact, that's what a lot of this book is about.

I used to get a lot of "sage" advice from guys who really knew the game. Guys who you'd be leaning on for every word. Guys like Sam Snead, Billy Casper, and Lee Trevino. Lee, in particular, was a guy I really came to know and respect. I found myself playing the game — and "feeling" about the game — in much the same way as he did. Lee taught me how to fade a tee shot effectively. Since I grew up as a right to left player

2

I don't think I could have made this change on my own. It really helps to establish a relationship like that. Someone you can turn to when things are really not going right at all, and you have to get it back in perspective.

But my relationship with my "peers" was just as important. Even though we're constantly in competition against one another, we helped each other. But let me explain this in a little more detail. You don't tell someone that he or she is making a bad move or is out of alignment unless you're asked. Don't volunteer advice. Also, if someone is playing really well, we didn't go up and say "Gee, Tom, your hand position at the top is just perfect." The next thing you know they'll start thinking about it and there goes their swing. Be helpful but be careful on advice.

Sure, you'll find the occasional pro who thinks he can get an advantage over everybody else by keeping his observations to himself, but that's the exception by far. Helping each other out is such a big part of the game, it's hard to single out any one in particular, but I'd say guys like Johnny Miller, J.C. Snead and Lanny Wadkins were the ones I could always rely on the most to set me straight when things started going haywire. You've got to have friends. It's important.

SECRET NO. 15: SINK THE SHORT ONES.

There are lots of things I could cover about how to practice your putting. The two things you should concentrate on are lag putting and sinking the short ones.

Lag putting is primarily a matter of feel, and feel is a matter of hand-eye coordination. Some of us are born with a little more or less than others, but whatever you've got can be improved upon. Practice long putts. Uphill. Downhill. Sidehill. Concentrate on distance control. Let these putts die at the hole.

In order to become a better short putter you must start by making the putts you know you can't miss and work back from there. The trick here is your subconscious. You want to program it with as many "successes" as you can. Start with one footers, square the blade and make solid contact. When you are ready to move back to two footers, pick an intermediate target one foot away and putt through it. On today's fast greens, the stroke you use for two-foot putts is exactly the same as one footers. In this way you will still be making one footers. Also, practice straight putts first and when you're ready to work on breaking putts, choose only those that break from right to left. This will prevent your stroke from getting into a cutting motion ... a danger if you dwell on left to right putts.

SECRET NO. 16: STRETCH DAILY.

Flexibility is so important to the game of golf that I can't overemphasize how important it is to establish a regular stretching routine that involves just about every part of your body.

Your best bet is to go through your stretching routine either in the morning or evening. Yes, as in every day! Stretching keeps your muscles long and lean and gives you the flexibility which is so vitally important to your game.

Now I'm not talking about simply lifting your hands above your head, counting to five and saying, "Well, that takes care of that." I'm talking about a well-established routine to cover every part of your body. There are a number of excellent stretching exercises that will take care of your fingers, hands, shoulders, back, hips and legs. And there are several good books that deal with stretching that can help you set up a daily program.

If you do stretch properly, and do it every day, you will definitely see a difference in your game.

SECRET NO. 17: STAMINA OVER STRENGTH.

As far as actual physical training to prepare yourself for playing the game, I'm a real advocate of developing "stamina over strength".

It's hard enough on the mind to make your way around a golf course — without having to worry about how your body is holding up. That's why it's so important to stay in good physical condition to play well. But you really don't have to overdo it.

Weight is one thing you should watch. Adults, as they begin to age, have a natural tendency to gain weight. This often makes them sluggish, which is not the way you want to be on a golf course. There are a number of different ways to keep your weight in check. A combination of proper diet and regular exercise is best.

Now, don't worry, I'm not about to suggest a strenuous exercise program. Quite frankly, I prefer the common sense approach ... Not too much, not too little. Gary Player was probably at the other end of the scale. He worked out all the time. He was known for it. And it worked for him. You need to get comfortable with what works for you. But you do need to exercise.

I'm also not an advocate of weight training because a bulky upper body can decrease your flexibility. Most successful golfers on the tour are not muscular at all. They're wiry, not bulked up. Don January was like that and he had a great deal of success over a very long career.

Leverage and swing speed are more important than strength when you hit the ball. If you're in the right position, loose, and using the right parts of your body to swing the club, you'll get the maximum speed that you're capable of getting. If you want to hit it longer, do what Couples, Love and John Daly do. Get loose. Develop your flexibility. Clubhead *speed* is what you're after, not brute force.

Some golfers jog two or three days a week. This along with stretching will help keep your muscles flexible and your stamina up. If you don't care for jogging, try walking, cycling, swimming, or any other activity that'll keep you loose and the blood running. While we're on the subject, it's not a bad idea to walk the golf course rather than use a cart. It's better exercise and it keeps you focused on the game.

SECRET No. 10

ESTABLISH A WARM-UP ROUTINE

Try to get to the course with enough time to stretch, swing a weighted club, and go through ten or fifteen minutes on the practice green. Hit five or six shots with each club, aiming each at a specific target. But don't spend too much time putting. You don't want your back to tighten up.

COMMIT TO PRACTICE

Success comes when you have confidence. Your swing is right, you feel comfortable, and you can "let it happen." You can only attain that mental state with practice, which means hard work. Develop a regular practice routine. Set up specific times. Work on your swing mechanics with a 6 or 7 iron. The more you practice, the more consistent your game will become.

SECRET No. 12

AIM IT

Once you're loose, start with a short iron and pick a target. Build up to your full swing but always practice shots toward a specific target. And work on your alignment and pre-shot position at all distances.

WHEN IT FEELS GOOD — STOP

If you're near the end of a practice or warm-up and you feel you're really in the groove — stop. End your practice on a positive note. If you only have five or ten balls left, leave them on the tee. You're out there to groove your swing, but don't overdo it.

25

SECRET No. 14

GET ANOTHER PAIR OF "EYES"

Sometimes it's good to get another perspective. You're doing something wrong but don't know what it is. Talk to someone familiar with your swing, someone you play with, and someone whose judgement you trust. That person can help get you back on track quickly.

SINK THE SHORT ONES

Start with one footers, square the blade and make solid contact. Program your subconscious with as many successes as you can. When you move to two footers, pick an intermediate target one foot away and putt through it. Use the same stroke for both. Practice straight putts first, then breaking putts, always going from right to left.

SECRET No. 16

STRETCH DAILY

Flexibility is important to your game. Establish a regular stretching routine involving every part of your body. Do it every day, in the morning or the evening. Stretching keeps your muscles long and lean, and you'll see the difference in your game once you're on a good program.

STAMINA OVER STRENGTH

Leverage and swing speed are more important than strength when you hit the ball. So it helps if you watch your weight and stay in good physical condition. You don't have to overdo it, but get on a regular exercise program and watch your diet. You don't need weight training, just a program to keep your muscles flexible, your stamina up and your weight down.

Part

3

The Secrets of Psychology & Mental Preparation

3

I've heard it said that once you've learned how to play, the game of Golf is about 95% mental. There's really a lot of truth to that.

I've already gone over how important it is to start by getting the right tools to fit your game. And then to get yourself in shape to play your best through the right kind of practice and physical conditioning.

But if you don't approach this game with the right mental attitude — then the perfect set of clubs, the most finely tuned body, and all the practice routines and instructional techniques in the world won't matter one bit.

So where do I start in giving you the real secrets the pros know when it comes to the "mental" part of the game? The biggest one is so obvious it may not seem like secret, but I think the secret is knowing that it's "number 1" ...

SECRET NO. 18: KEEP IT IN PERSPECTIVE.

The way I look at it is the way just about every other successful pro looks at it ... Golf is a "game," pure and simple. And when you play a game, you like to have fun. How many other professions are there where you can make a living by playing a game? I don't like to work. I'd rather play. So I make my work play. Whistling down the fairway ... taking in the scenery ... You just don't have to take it all so seriously!

Even the guys who seem to be the most serious players during a round will tell you when it's all over that they were having fun out there. Lee Trevino and Jack Nicklaus are probably the two best examples to illustrate this point. Everybody knows Lee projects himself in the most relaxed, carefree manner on the golf course ... but even Jack, the most outwardly intense player you might imagine, would reveal that he's at his best when he's having a good time.

You might have to start by consciously working at it, like everything else. Step back during a round. Look around. Feel the breeze. Listen to the birds. But you can't force it. It's only when this overall attitude toward golf becomes as natural to you as taking a breath of fresh air that you will see those strokes start dropping from your scorecard.

SECRET NO. 19: EVEN OUT THE HIGHS AND LOWS.

A big-money pro knows how important it is to stay on an emotionally level track throughout his round. No shot is any more or less important than any other shot. If you're hitting your approach to the green on "number 3" — or putting for a birdie on "17" — it has exactly the same value. It is one stroke.

Johnny Miller and I were paired together one day when he hit a tremendous shot from 225 yards out to within 3 feet of the hole. The gallery went crazy and it pumped

3

Johnny up so much that he hit the putt dead center, but so hard that it bounced over the top of the hole. He lost that tournament by one stroke. When we talked about what happened later on, he realized the importance of not letting the gallery or the success or failure of one shot affect the next.

Let's face it. It's very easy for the average golfer to let his round get completely away from him just because of one poorly played shot. But when you're a pro, that simply *can't* happen! There are eighteen holes to be played. You can never let a particularly bad shot — or for that matter, a particularly good shot — affect the way you will play the next one.

I think Fred Couples is one of the most successful players on the tour today, in terms of maintaining a consistent emotional level. If you watch him carefully, you will never know whether he's ten strokes in the lead, or twenty strokes back.

The next time you play a poor shot — or for that matter, a good one — consciously erase it from your mind, and immediately begin thinking about how you will play the next one. Not worrying about one stroke can easily save you five or six others.

SECRET NO. 20: FIND YOUR OWN GAME AND *PLAY* IT!

I'm always hearing something like this from the average golfer ... "Jerry, I can't seem to hit the ball down the middle of the fairway. It always wants to go left. How do I correct this?" Well, what I say to them is this ... "Aim to the right of the fairway. Your ball will end up in the middle."

Sounds simple, but it illustrates a very key philosophy in the way every pro on the tour plays the game. They play it *their* way. They don't try and force the ball to go straight if they're getting a natural draw from the ball. They just aim a little to the right and let it happen!

Every pro "works" the ball one way or the other. Some like to draw it. Some like to fade it. So depending on how they play, they aim to the right, or aim to the left. All they've got to think about is how to align themselves to the left or right of the target — and then whack it! (And we'll talk more about alignment in later chapters).

And by the way, you've got to have confidence that your ball will move the way you expect it to move. That's why you've got to play it *your* way. Think about all those guys who have to send the ball out over the water at Pebble Beach in order to hit the green. They *know* it'll come back for them, because that's the way they play it.

The point is, it's harder to hit a straight ball than any other. So why bother trying? Find out how *you* tend to play it ... and *play* it! Johnny Miller was the only guy I ever saw who hit a straight ball. He hit it dead straight. There may have been others before or after my time, but he was the only one I saw. He'd aim straight, and he'd hit it straight ... The only one.

3

SECRET NO. 21: PREPARE YOURSELF AND "LET IT FLY."

When you get right down to it, actually striking the ball is the easiest part of the game. What you really have to do is completely prepare yourself *before* you hit ... and then just let it happen!

Actually, I like to think of it as "programming yourself." It kind of starts with a built-in confidence that you will execute your swing in the same way you've performed it over and over again through countless hours of practice and competition.

Along with this confidence, you add a solid pre-shot routine for judging the situation, the distance, the weather conditions, and the lie ... you determine the proper club, grip, alignment, stance, and swing key — until you are satisfied that everything has been taken care of up until the moment you are ready to pull the trigger ...

Then, you do it.

Most of the time, I don't even consciously feel myself swinging the club. Everything has already been taken care of. The more you prepare yourself before a shot, the less you will be "thinking" during a shot ... and the lower you will score!

The pros have all sorts of pre-shot routines they use over and over again to get them in this state of mind. If anything should happen to distract them at any time during this routine, they will stop the routine and start all over again from the very beginning.

One pro that sticks out in my mind is Billy Casper. His routine would start by figuring out what club to use, then he'd pull the club out of the bag, take two practice swings, set up, and let fly. If anything happened to disrupt his concentration during that routine, he would actually *put the club back in the bag*, pull it out again, and continue right along with his routine. He's the only guy I ever saw go to that extreme. Anybody else would step back and say, "Keep the baby quiet," or whatever and then go ahead. He'd actually put the club back in the bag. And I'll tell you, Billy was a heady golfer. One of the best in the world. So is that going too far? Sometimes I think I would have been better off to do it too.

SECRET NO. 22: FOCUS IN — FOCUS OUT.

A lot has been said about the pro's amazing ability to concentrate as much as he does through 18 holes of competitive golf.

You want to know the secret? Don't try. The average golfer spends four, almost five hours at a time on a golf course. And nowadays it's sadly almost as long of an eternity on the golf tour. There's simply no way to maintain a constant level of concentration for that long of a time. No way.

The way to get through a round is by continually focusing in — and focusing out as you play. And it's really not as tough as it sounds. It begins as you take your shot ... (That's the time I've already talked about — when you swing without actually thinking about it).

3

... You immediately begin to take in the result. Good, bad, or indifferent. You start walking toward your ball, developing a plan of how you will play your next shot. The closer you get to your ball, the more you are studying the situation, the more you are preparing yourself for the next shot. By the time you are at the address position and ready to pull the trigger, you have completely analyzed the situation and have determined exactly how you will execute the shot. It is at this precise moment that you FOCUS IN. You focus on your key swing thought and nothing else gets in your mind for the next 2 or 3 seconds.

Some pros refer to it as "the zone." In the past, I've thought about it as if I were flicking on a light switch at the same moment I'm starting my backswing. But the important thing to think about is that you aren't thinking about any negatives or any "what ifs." You've programmed yourself to do the right thing, and now you're doing it. Any thought during that stroke can only interfere with what is already "plugged-in" in your own mind.

They used to call me "dial-tone" on the tour, because I had the ability to go completely blank. I had *no* thought. Zippo.

When you're really in the zone, you're constantly flicking that light switch on and off. Everything's working. And you're really having a good time doing it.

SECRET NO. 23: VISUALIZE A POSITIVE RESULT.

The power of the mind is tremendous. For my money, there is no other sport where this is more evident than in the game of golf. Positive thinking is one thing. But I will suggest a technique the pros use that takes it a giant step further ...

Visualization.

Visualization is what we do before we stand up to hit each and every golf shot ... We stand directly behind the ball and the target ... We imagine the impact of the club hitting the ball ... We see the gentle arc of the ball in the air ... We witness the ball hitting the surface of the green ... We watch as it bounces and rolls toward the pin ... We see it follow the contours of the green as it approaches the cup ... And we see it deftly strike the pin and vanish into the hole.

And remember this important key — the more vividly detailed you picture this happening in your mind, the more successful you will be.

Now all this may sound like pretty weird stuff, but when you think about it, it makes a lot of sense. What I've mentioned before about "focusing out" is really a form of clearing your mind of all negative thinking. It's those "voices" ... "Don't hit it to the left" ... "Don't swing too hard" ... "Don't screw this up." These are the things that tense you up and make a shot go bad. When you take the time to "visualize" a successfully executed shot in a very detailed way, you are actually replacing those negative thoughts with a solid positive thought ... pushing those negative thoughts out of the way. Believe me, it works!

3

You can't really discuss visualization in golf without mentioning Jack Nicklaus. I've seen Jack perform near supernatural acts. I've watched his ball break uphill on a putt to go in the hole ... on the exact same line as my putt. Mine broke away!

I was paired with Jack at the Colonial NIT in Fort Worth, Texas, one year and he was having a tough time with his right-to-left swing. As you know Jack likes to hit a fade whenever he can. It's the more comfortable shot for him. On the 10th hole this day, a tough par 4, the wind was blowing left to right and you just can't let it get too far on the right side or you'll get blocked out by some huge trees. For control, the hole demanded a draw. As I said, Jack wasn't making very good swings when he tried to "turn it over."

What he did in this case was convince his own mind that the wind was blowing right to left (the perfect condition for a fade), aimed left and put his best swing on the ball. He hit a great tee shot! He changed the real conditions into more pleasing conditions in his mind which allowed him to play to his own strengths.

SECRET NO. 24: COMPETE, AND PLAY TO WIN!

The last secret I'll cover about the mental part of the game is that, like any other game, you're supposed have to fun ... but, above all, you're supposed to *win*!

It's easy for the pros to keep that "winning" attitude in mind. After all, it's our bread and butter. But what about the average, or maybe above average golfer like you? How do you get that competitive feeling and use it to shave those strokes off your card?

The first thing I, or any pro, would tell you is "stop taking those 'mulligans.' Quit playing 'winter rules.' And start putting the ball into the hole *every time*!" There are no "gimmies" in competitive golf. So when you're out playing in your Sunday foursome, you've got to play it by the rules. It may cost you a few strokes in the short run, but it'll help get you in the right frame of mind to play *every* shot, because every shot *counts*! And in the long run your score will be better for it.

The next thing I would tell you is to simply "start competing!" Enter those club tournaments ... the association get-togethers ... the company outings. There is no substitute for regular, old-fashioned competition to build confidence and a positive mental attitude toward the game.

It always seems more important when it really counts. When you've had little experience with truly competitive golf, that first shot off the first tee with everybody watching is always the most difficult shot to hit. "Please, God, just let me hit it in the air this one time!" The more you compete, the more you will overcome the fears, the more you learn to relax and play the game the way it was meant to be played. The way it's *fun* to play!

You'll start to realize, "Hey, these guys aren't worried about me, and how I'll hit my tee shot. They're thinking about their own tee shot! So what's the big deal? I've got it down. I'm prepared. So I'm just going to let it fly. If it's good, that's great. If it's not good, well that's great too. I'll just start thinking about my next shot, walk down that first fairway, take in the beauty and excitement of the day ahead, and have myself a "good ole time!"

SECRET No. 18

KEEP IT IN PERSPECTIVE

Golf is a "game," pure and simple. And when you play a game, you like to have fun. You might start out by consciously working at it, like everything else. But take time to step back during a round. Feel the breeze. Listen to the birds. Don't take it all so seriously.

EVEN OUT THE
HIGHS AND LOWS

Always remember, no shot is any more or less important than any other shot. Whether you're hitting your approach to the green on number 3 — or putting for a birdie on 17 — it has exactly the same value. It is one stroke.

SECRET No. 20

FIND YOUR OWN GAME
AND *PLAY* IT

Every pro "works" the ball one way or the other. Some like to draw it. Some like to fade it. Don't worry about hitting a "straight" ball every time. Find out how you naturally play the ball . . . and *play* it!

PREPARE YOURSELF AND "LET IT FLY"

Actually striking the ball is the easiest part of the game. What you have to do is completely "program" yourself before you hit it. Start with the confidence of hours of practice and experience . . . determine the right club, grip, alignment, stance, etc. . . . and then just pull the trigger! The less you "think" during a shot, the lower you will score.

SECRET No. 22

FOCUS IN — FOCUS OUT

A pro is continually focusing in, and focusing out during a round . . . calmly thinking about all the factors involved in playing the next shot — until the moment *before* actually triggering the swing. In that instant all the negatives and "what ifs" have been washed away.

VISUALIZE A
POSITIVE RESULT

Before you hit your golf shot, stand behind it and visualize in the most vivid way possible how it will look as it flies through the air, hits the ground, and softly rolls toward the target. This type of positive imagery actually acts to replace all those negative thoughts you *really* want to avoid as you're standing over your shot.

SECRET No. 24

COMPETE, AND PLAY TO WIN

The pros know how important it is to maintain a "winning" attitude. Always play the game as a true competitor, and it will surely be reflected in your scorecard when it really counts. And that means no "mulligans" off the first tee — and finishing off every hole.

Part

The Secrets of Knowing & Managing The Course

4

Okay, so now you've got the tools you need, and you're physically and mentally prepared to play the game. Now you're ready to walk up to the first tee and whack it. Right?

Wrong.

As important as the warm-ups, practice, and physical and mental preparation are, there are a few more things the average golfer takes for granted before starting his round that end up costing valuable strokes on the scorecard.

I'm going to tell you how a tour player and his caddy prepare themselves to play a golf course and what you can use out of that process to lower your scores. In golf you play the course, not your fellow competitor. Knowing the course is like knowing your opponent. Understanding your tendencies, your personal golf strengths and weaknesses, and fitting your game into the golf course each time is simple common sense.

SECRET NO. 25: KNOW THE COURSE.

Does your golf course have a scorecard with a course map printed on it? If so, look at it and determine which direction each hole plays. Draw lines or arrows across the map to indicate the direction of the prevailing winds. This will really help you in making smart club decisions on the course. Particularly when you're blocked by trees and throwing a little grass in the air is useless.

Secondly, direction can help you read greens. If you are in the southern United States and play in Bermuda grass greens, which can be very grainy, that grass tends to grow toward the setting sun. Which direction is west on your course?

Course conditions change from time to time, particularly from season to season. Knowing that the fairways are hard or soft can make the difference in whether you blow a driver through the dogleg or choose a 3 wood instead. If your superintendent is letting the rough grow, it may be in your best interest to leave a long iron at home in favor of a 5 wood or possibly one of the "Baffler" or "Railer" woods especially designed to get a ball up and out of deep grass.

Furthermore, with respect to equipment, do you carry the right wedges for your course? If your course is mowed tightly you're going to have a tough time using a sand wedge from the fairway if it has a lot of bounce. If the sand in your bunkers is fluffy and relatively deep, a high degree of bounce and a nice wide flange on your sand wedge will be helpful. Do you need both types? If your greens are slick and built with a lot of undulation, a 60° wedge or lob wedge might save you some strokes.

One last thought on knowing the course or courses you regularly play. Make sure you carry the right clubs for the par 3's on your course. If you've got a 200 yarder and don't hit your long irons with confidence, this could be justification for carrying that 4 wood.

It's true that you don't have to go to all this trouble in order to have fun playing golf and Lord knows, I want you to have fun, but if you're interested in posting lower scores

4

and getting your handicap down to a single digit, these techniques are worth it.

SECRET NO. 26: KNOW THE DISTANCE.

Think about the yardages on your course for a moment. Know how your course and any new or unfamiliar course you're going to play is marked. Many courses use 150 yard markers such as stakes or bushes. Others have markers at 125 and 175 yard distances. Still other courses mark the tops of their sprinkler heads. Are these distances measured to the front or middle of the green? Are they accurate? What about the distance from a given tee box on your course to a sand trap or water hazard near the landing area? Do you really know how far you need to carry the ball to clear it or what the safe lay up distance is? Step it off sometime. Then you'll *know*. You can check the other distance markers for accuracy this way, too.

The yardage books courses sell nowadays are usually very good. If you're fortunate enough to play at a course where the PGA Tour stops, you may be able to get "The Book." "The Book" is a yardage book prepared by George Lucas and updated for any course changes. No player or caddy I know of goes on a tournament course without "The Book" and they still check and step off the distances.

SECRET NO. 27: KNOW THE HOLE.

The importance of knowledge comes even more into play when we're talking about each individual hole.

A tour pro would never attempt to play a hole in a tournament before actually playing it in practice rounds in the days leading up to the tournament. What we are doing is figuring out the best way to play the hole. We're looking for a good landing area for our tee shot, a good angle of approach to the green. We are checking the distances in our yardage books.

We are also looking for those places on certain holes where you just can't hit it. You know, alligator country ... where you wouldn't go even to look for your own children. These are the places where you change your game, if necessary, in order to avoid them. Don't get so afraid of these places that you can't swing, but know they are there; play away from them and avoid the huge numbers on the scorecard.

Most of your golf is probably played on one or two courses. Know the holes on these courses as well as you can.

When you play a new or unfamiliar course, study the scoreboard and yardage book. Be aware and be wary of "blind shots" either on tee shots or approaches. Ride or walk to the top of the hill, if possible, and check out the target. At least look at the card and see what it shows is lurking beyond that hill.

Asking advice from your playing partner can be helpful, against the rules, and/or dangerous. If it's a friendly match and no one really cares, ask someone more familiar with the hole what to expect. Ask about distance in terms of yardage though. If you ask what club you should use, you may get some well intended but bad information for your game. A 5 iron is not a 5 iron, you know. Your partner may hit his 5 iron 10 to 20 yards longer or shorter than you. Plus, depending on the manufacturer, there can be a significant difference from the 5 iron in one set and the 5 iron in a seemingly identical set. The U.S.G.A. prohibits asking your opponent for this kind of advice, so if you're in a tournament and/or your group plays according to the strict rules, asking for advice is not allowed.

SECRET NO. 28: PLAY YOUR OWN GAME.

As long as we're discussing the subject of asking for advice, this is probably the best time to mention the importance of playing your own game. There is no more important message in this book than knowing and playing your own game. What are your strengths and weaknesses? What is your normal ball flight? Left to right? Right to left? How much?

I learned a great deal from Sam Snead and Lee Trevino as I was coming up. But my swing and my game are nothing like theirs. In fact, they aren't even similar to one another. You can learn from others but not necessarily copy their style of swing or their approach to the game. Develop your own style, based on whatever feels natural and comfortable to you. Once you make a commitment to developing your own game it doesn't make much sense to abandon it at a critical moment during a match. Right?

I was painfully reminded of this simple principle one day early in my career when I was playing a round with Jack Nicklaus. There was a deep bunker guarding the approach to the green on a mid-length par 5, and I had already decided that I would lay up and set myself up for a nice easy chip to the green. Jack hit first. And Jack's shot sailed twenty yards over the trap, and nestled itself right up close to the pin. Super shot. I thought to myself, "Hey, I'm a big hitter. If Jack can do that so can I. I'll just put my approach right up there next to Jack's." Out of the trap in three, long log putt for four and white knuckle 3-footer for par. Jack made eagle.

Let me repeat. Don't ever, EVER, let the way someone else is playing influence your own style of play. Always play your own game.

SECRET NO. 29: PLAY THE PERCENTAGES.

Speaking of Jack Nicklaus, let me just say this. I think Jack is the best there ever was as far as managing a golf course. He's in a class by himself. How does he do it?

4

Simple. He's a master at playing the percentages.

By that I mean, Jack is always thinking. He can size up a situation better than just about anybody else I've ever seen and come up with the "right" way to play it under the given circumstances. And the "right" way is almost always the way that will potentially put him in the least amount of trouble. Now don't get me wrong, I'm not saying that Jack is "conservative." What I'm saying is that at any given time, he knows the score. He knows what's at stake. He knows that a poor result in a particular situation could lead to even more trouble. Or, that the conditions are right to go for it, without "letting the horse out of the barn."

Arnold Palmer, of course, went the other way. He was aggressive. He was exciting. But he was a gambler. His amazing talent carried him through in most cases. But can you think of any successful tour player who made as many double and triple bogies as Arnie? Now my feeling is that you probably don't have quite the talent of Arnold Palmer, so you're not going to have the ability he did to recover from trouble once you get into it, or make up for it with eagles and birdies elsewhere.

Hit fairways and greens and the score will take care of itself. Don't try to fire at every pin. Play to the pins your natural shape of shot favors. Don't overwork the ball. Very few guys on tour are working every other shot this way and that. They play shots which allow themselves to play their most natural shot. When the match dictates that you *must* gamble ... hitch up your pants (Palmer style) and go for it!

SECRET NO. 30: CUSTOMIZE YOUR STRATEGY.

Ever go out to the range on a Saturday morning for your weekly match with the gang and feel like you must be using someone else's body? Nothing feels right. Your hands won't fit onto the club, you can't make a decent turn ... your gentle draw has turned into big banana ball.

Don't panic. Check your alignment and ball position first but even if you can't find your old groove you're going to be okay.

What you need to do for that day and that round is play with what you've got. Aim and allow for your "new" left to right ball flight until it shows signs of getting back to normal. Don't fight it. Play it.

A lot of good rounds of tournament golf have been posted by guys who didn't really have their best game on a given day. Everyone has those days. It's how well you react to this kind of adversity that determines what kind of golfer you are. In fact, I have a more satisfied feeling about those rounds than the ones on days when everything I did was right. And friend, you're going to have a lot more scrambling days than others.

4

SECRET NO. 31: DON'T GET PSYCHED OUT.

What makes some holes harder than others? The length, the hazards, the size of the green? Yes, each of these can contribute to our attitude about a hole. When you feel the need to "kill" it off the tee, you tense up and hit one of your worst drives. When you try to avoid the sand in front of the green, you pull up and out of the swing early, trying to "help" it up and over. When we let these shots psyche us out of making our normal natural swings, we're working against ourselves.

What kind of holes do the pros think are the hardest to play? Generally, par 3's. Because you've only got one shot to get it on the green and in the best position to putt. What are the easiest holes? Par 5's. There you've got three chances to make at least two good shots. If you mess up your drive, you can always get it back with a good second shot and approach.

You also always have to consider the conditions of a hole each time you play it. The 12th hole at Augusta is about the best example I can think of. One year I played it with Miller Barber. He was up first, with a 6 iron in his hand. Hit the ball perfectly. Looked like the wind was going to pull it right in toward the hole. All of a sudden, one of the crazy swirls of wind around that hole caught it, and dropped it in the middle of Rae's Creek. I had already decided I was going to hit a 6 iron, too. And I did. Hit it exactly the same way Miller did. But my ball drifted in and landed right by the hole. How do you figure? If I'd hit first, I'd have been the one in the water. The conditions just make that a funny hole to play. You've got to be aware of those things.

Here's a tip the tour pros use. There are always particular holes you don't like to play. There's just something about them that always comes up and grabs you. And then there are the holes that you're always scoring well on for one reason or another. Sometime when you're playing one of those holes you don't like, think about a hole you do like that's about the same distance. Pretend *that's* the hole you're actually playing. The clearer you visualize that other hole, the better it works.

SECRET No. 25

KNOW THE COURSE

If a course map is printed on your scorecard, determine which direction each hole plays. Then determine wind direction. Know if the fairways are hard or soft, the condition of the bunker sand, if the rough has deep grass, or if the greens are slick. This knowledge will help you make smart decisions on the course.

KNOW THE DISTANCE

Marked distances vary on courses. So before you set foot on the course, find out how it's marked and where the markers are. Know if the distances are marked to the front or middle of the green, the distance from the tee box to a sand trap or a water hazard, and if the distances are accurate. Step off a measured distance to determine accuracy.

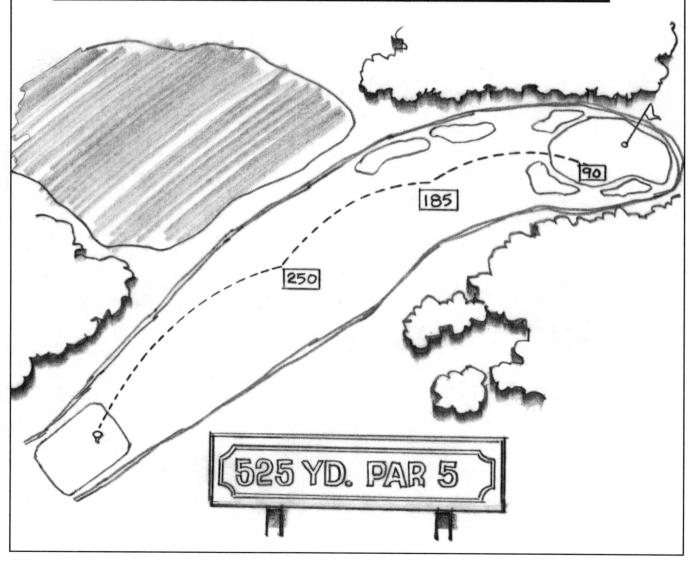

SECRET No. 27

KNOW THE HOLE

If possible, play the course prior to playing a tournament. And take notes. When playing a hole, look for a good landing area for a tee shot and a good angle approach to the green. Look for the places on each hole where you just can't hit the ball. Always be aware of the blind shots. During a round, use your yardage book or check from the top of the hill — to determine what lies beyond the hill.

SECRET No. 28

PLAY YOUR OWN GAME

Understand your strengths and weaknesses. Determine the shape of your normal shot, whether it's left to right or right to left. You can learn from others, but don't simply copy their approach to the game or their style of swing. Play your own game.

SECRET No. 29

PLAY THE PERCENTAGES

Always size up the situation as you move along the course. Hit fairways and greens and let the score take care of itself. Don't fire at every pin and don't overwork the ball. Play shots that allow you to play your most natural shot. Only go against the odds when the match dictates that you must gamble to win.

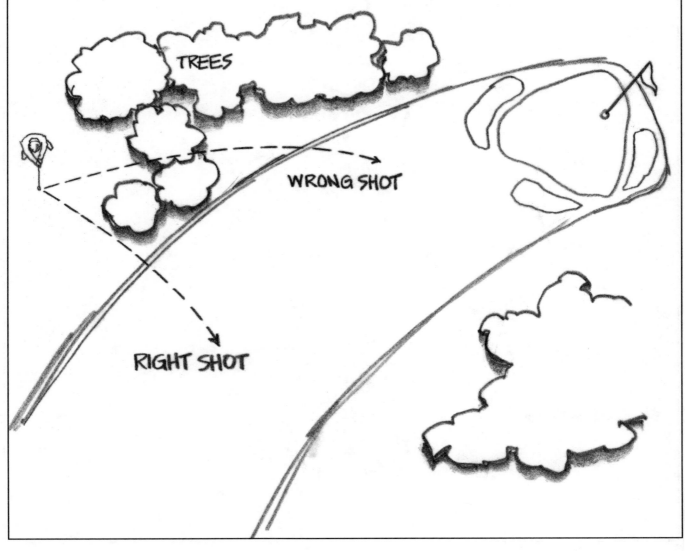

TREES

WRONG SHOT

RIGHT SHOT

CUSTOMIZE YOUR STRATEGY

If you can't find your groove on a given day, don't panic. Play with what you've got, which may be more than you think. Aim and allow for your "new" ball flight until you can see signs that you're getting back to normal. Don't fight it. Play it. Remember, everyone has those days.

SECRET No. 31

DON'T GET PSYCHED OUT

Some holes are harder than others, partially because of the size of the green or the hazards. But another reason is that golfers tense up when they approach these troublesome holes. They psyche themselves out. When you get to a hole you don't like, stop for a moment and relax. Think about a hole you like to play. Then pretend that's the hole you're actually playing.

Part

5

The Secrets of
The Basics

In order to take full advantage of the more advanced aspects of this book, you must first have a thorough understanding and command of the basic mechanical sequence of the swing. One of the huge advantages the accomplished touring pro has over most other golfers is, we don't have to spend much time thinking about mechanics during a round. Our swings are more or less in our subconscious mind. We are thinking about playing golf, not how to make a golf swing.

The more you can do this, the better player you will become. But you must have good, repeatable mechanics as a basis. The better your basics, the fewer compensations you have to make. I think it might be valuable for you to know and understand what's really taking place during the golf swing and what factors govern which results.

The five Ball Flight Laws are the fundamentals governing the flight, or in the case of a putt, the roll, of all shots. The Ball Flight Laws are:

- Clubhead Speed is the velocity of the clubhead through the air, measured at the moment of impact.

- Clubhead Path is the direction the clubhead is moving at the moment of impact.

- Clubface Angle is the degree to which the clubface is or isn't square to the clubhead path at impact. Note, not in relation to the target line.

- Angle of Approach is the degree to which the clubhead is descending or ascending at the moment of impact.

- Center of Mass is how close to the center of the mass of the clubhead contact with the ball occurs.

Direction of ball flight is governed by clubface angle, clubhead path and the centeredness of impact. Distance and trajectory are influenced primarily by clubhead speed, angle of approach and again, the centeredness of impact.

The better your basics, the more closely you will come to "perfection" with respect to the Ball Flight Laws. Does this mean that the guy with the best mechanics is always the best player? Obviously not. Usually, the best player is the one with the most repeatable swing. If your swing repeats, your ball flight repeats. And if you know where your ball is going all the time, it's just a matter of pointing it in the right direction and choosing the right club. Ho hum, what a simple game.

SECRET NO. 32: TRUST YOUR CLUB SELECTION.

You've heard the expression "Let the club do the work"? This is what I'm talking about here. If you've judged the distance properly, and you know your own capabilities through all your practice, you should *know* you've got the right club for the job. You should have no indecision whatsoever about what you've got in your hands while you're standing over the ball. You'll be ready to make a smooth, natural stroke at it.

SECRET NO. 33: DON'T UNDERCLUB.

I see it all the time. Guys get up to the tee on a long par 3 with an iron in their hand when they should be using a wood — trying to hit a 3 iron from the rough when they can be using a 4 wood. I guess it's got something to do with a "macho" thing. But nothing is more stupid and less macho than a guy obviously trying to be macho. He's got no chance anyway. *Always* give yourself enough club. They use the term in putting, but it works just as well for any shot in golf . . . "Never up, never in."

Also, most courses are designed with the bunkers and hazards toward the front of the greens. They put all that trouble up there to catch the weak shots. Be smart. Don't play directly against the strength of the golf course.

SECRET NO. 34: GET A GRIP — AND STAY WITH IT!

I use the Vardon or overlapping grip, but the two other generally accepted grips — the interlocking and the ten-finger or baseball grip — are occasionally used. Jack Nicklaus and Tom Kite have both had successful careers using the interlocking method. Since a good grip is a passive thing rather than an active thing in the sequence of the swing, the position of the little finger of the right hand is not of major consequence. It's okay to experiment to see which method feels best to you but once you decide, work on perfecting that method instead of changing it all the time.

SECRET NO. 35: LOSE CONTROL TO GAIN CONTROL.

The real keys to a good grip accomplish two things: (1) a good grip returns the clubface at impact to the same position it held at address, and (2) the hands and wrists must be relaxed and flexible enough that they do not inhibit the speed of the clubhead through impact. With an excellent grip such as Hogan's, Nelson's, and a few others, virtually no in-stroke compensations are made with the small muscles of the hands or wrists during the backswing and downswing in order to accomplish the two main objectives. In average to poor players, the squaring of the clubface is left almost entirely up to the last second adjustment of the hands. This will be clearer a little later in this chapter.

The "V's" of each hand, as shown in the illustrations, should point to the same right shoulder position. This means the hands are in a complementary position, working together as a unit. The butt end of the club should be under the heel pad of the left hand. If it moves down into the palm under the thumb pad, you'll lose control. The club is held in the fingers of the right hand, and the padded portion of the right hand just below the index finger should be pressing gently against the shaft of the club. You should feel that the hands are working as one throughout the swing, not pulling apart or a feeling of dominance by one hand or the other. In fact, once you have taken your grip, you will want to feel the weight of the clubhead rather than the pressure of the grip. A safecracker's touch … light, light, light.

SECRET NO. 36: ADDRESS THE BALL NATURALLY.

As mentioned in the chapter on practice, use a 6 or 7 iron when working on your mechanics. With this kind of club you will want to have your feet slightly less than shoulder-width apart. Your weight should be evenly distributed between the feet and centered between the ball and heel of the foot. Add a little flex to your knees but avoid the tendency to squat down. Stand tall to the ball. We are going to make a tilted circular motion with the club during the swing, so to best support that arc or swing plane you need to tilt your body into an accommodating position. Rather than leaning over toward the ball with your upper body, I want you to move your pelvis back … out from underneath your shoulders. Look at my setup position in the illustration and compare your position. I recommend you use a full-length mirror so you can actually see your posture. Your back should remain fairly straight and your head should be up. By this I mean your chin should not have dropped down onto your chest.

From the side, a good setup position looks balanced. Draw an imaginary line vertically from the tips of your shoes up. The front of your shoulders should just touch this line. Your head and your posterior should counter-balance one another.

Now then, let's see if we can put the grip and posture together and create a good golf setup position. Begin by getting a good grip out in front of you, with your hands directly in front of your face at about arm's length. Then, with your knees already flexed and your feet at the proper width, allow your extended arms to drop slowly. As the backs of your elbows make contact with your body, allow your upper body to bend into the same good posture you practiced earlier. When the clubhead makes contact with the ground, you're there. From the front you should see a "Y" formed by the shaft of the club and the angle of the two arms. This won't quite be a symmetrical position because the right and left hand don't join on the club in the exact same place.

SECRET NO. 37: PLACE THE BALL IN THE RIGHT POSITION.

What is really key here is that you don't create unnatural angles in your set up. The shaft of the club should be perpendicular to the alignment of your shoulders, and the head of the club and your hands should be on a line about two inches inside your left

5

heel. From the side, your arms are almost vertical in a relaxed and natural hanging position from your shoulders.

The width of the stance varies from club to club, but the relationship between the ball position and the left foot remains constant for all standard shots. As you swing the club, the clubhead is making an arc or circle in the air. The low point in this arc is the point at which we want to contact the ball. As you move the right foot away from the left for the longer clubs, an interesting but natural thing happens: your center of gravity moves to the right slightly and the arc of the swinging clubhead is widened. Both of these natural adjustments work to your advantage in making shots with the longer clubs. Having the head more over the ball on the shorter shots and having the feet closer together, assists you in making a steeper descent and a sharper blow into the ball on short irons. By adjusting your stance you don't need to try to make a different swing with different clubs.

SECRET NO. 38: FIRST THE TARGET — THEN THE BALL.

The best way I know to get yourself in really good alignment (hardly anything else you do in setting up for a shot is more important than this) is to do it Jack's way.

Get behind the ball on the target line. Draw an imaginary line to your target. Pick out an intermediate target within two or three feet along that line in front of your ball. When you step to the side of the ball to get into your setup position, keep your eyes on the intermediate target and align your clubface to that target.

One clue here that many beginning golfers don't know: the bottom edge of your irons and the top of the clubface of your wood clubs represent the aiming edge for those clubs.

Once you have squared the clubface to the target line you only need to square your body to the clubface. Until your feet are in place, don't move the clubface again. Once your body is in position, you should relax, waggle the club, and begin your swing in a smooth flowing sequence, without any physical or mental interruptions.

SECRET NO. 39: ONE PIECE, ONE MOVING PART.

Okay, the hard part, the real technical positioning of the golf swing is over and we can move on to the fun part. I like the phrase "a one piece take away" because although, in reality, there is a slight lag between the initial motion of the club, hands, arms, shoulders, hips and legs into the full turn of the backswing, if you can get it into a single sequence instead of a series of parts, you will be miles ahead. Try not to get too caught up into the structure of the backswing or a perfect position at the top. You don't hit the ball with your backswing. It is only preparing you for the downswing.

SECRET NO. 40: LET THE LARGE MUSCLES LEAD.

What you want to accomplish is a kind of "bottom-up" coiling. You want your big muscles to control the movement of the club, not the hands or arms. As Sam Snead used to tell me, "Get your left arm against your left breast and keep it there." This keeps the club on plane throughout the swing. As the large muscles of the body are turning to the right, you should feel a natural transference of weight to the inside of the right knee. It is important that the right knee stay flexed and in nearly the same position as it started from at address throughout the backswing motion.

SECRET NO. 41: DON'T HINGE ... COCK!

Make a nice wide arc with the clubhead by keeping a relaxed extension in the arms. Sometimes I like to think about pulling away from the target line with the right hand a little bit. This seems to keep me from picking up the club. As you practice the mechanics of the basic swing, you should be aware that the wrists do not hinge from side to side during any part of the stroke. This means that at address the back of your left hand is more or less facing the target. And if you do not manipulate the club left or right with the hands during the backswing, your hand position will look the same to you at the top as it did at address. If you should draw a straight line between the palms of your hands, that line will always point to the center of your body, throughout the swing. Since this is important to understand, let me describe it a different way. Keep your thumbs on top of the club at address and at impact; and directly underneath the club at the top of your backswing and at the full extent of your follow through.

SECRET NO. 42: YOUR LOWER BODY TRIGGERS THE DOWNSWING.

During the change of direction — or, as some prefer to call it, the top of the backswing — the photographers can capture what appears to be a set position. All of the great players over the years have been photographed in this position and the comparisons have been made between them. In truth, there is no top of the backswing. At the same moment the upper body has completed its coil, the lower body is already into its forward or left turning motion. The most important thing here is that the large muscles of the body make the backswing rather than just the arms and hands. And that the majority of the weight of the body is gathered in a balanced position toward the inside of the right knee.

This is the real moment of truth in the golf swing. However you begin your downswing, in terms of position, balance and initial direction of movement will determine

5

everything else to follow. Your swing must be pre-programmed because adjustments during the downswing are virtually impossible.

My friend, Ken Venturi, would remind me that if you move, move laterally, not up and down, during the swing. A great deal of inconsistency occurs in the beginners' swing when they allow their knees to straighten and re-flex, or their spine angle to move from the good tilted position to the vertical position during the backswing or follow through.

SECRET NO. 43: GO LEFT, YOUNG MAN, LEFT.

You know that the lower body has already started its move into the downswing ahead of the upper body. But where is it going? "Left, young man, left." Turn your left hip left, not toward the target. We don't want a lateral slide, we want a turn. We want a turn of the hips that will result in the right hip actually ending up closer to the target than the left hip at the full follow through. A little bit of lateral movement is okay but don't make a big slide toward the target.

SECRET NO. 44: EXTEND "THROUGH" THE BALL.

I'm going to tell you a couple of secrets here that Sam Snead and Byron Nelson gave to me. But I want to put these thoughts in proper context. Neither were advocating an independent action of the arms. Rather, they were describing a reaction of the arms to a good swing and turning motion of the body. Byron emphasized keeping the right arm as close to the body as possible during the downswing and impact. This creates a very powerful position and a position of great leverage on the ball. Sam liked to think about the left arm breaking down after impact so the right arm could straighten naturally and extend toward the target. If the left arm stays straight too long through impact the left wrist will break down. If the left arm folds naturally at the elbow immediately after impact then the left wrist will remain firm and straight and the clubface will stay square.

I think this is a wonderful swing thought, too, because it really illustrates the proper swing plane. From inside, in the first half of the downswing, to inside, in the second half or the follow through. The determining factor in that circular swinging motion is the coiling and uncoiling of the body, the large muscles. The arms, wrists and hands must remain relaxed and reactive to the turning motion rather than taking on independent activities of their own.

SECRET NO. 45: BALANCE YOUR SWING.

Throughout the golf swing, maintaining good balance is an important key. If you tend to lose your balance out over your toes during the swing, your shots will tend to go left. If you tend to lose your balance falling back, your shots probably go right. The "fire and fall back" move, also known as the reverse weight shift, is a killer move. You really can't make a decent golf swing if your weight is moving to the right side during impact. For the better players who are plagued by the occasional snap hook, think about this: don't swing the club any faster than you can turn your shoulders. This will keep the butt end of the club pointing more or less at the center of your body through impact . . . square to the target.

SECRET NO. 46: FIND YOUR OWN TEMPO.

Just a word or two on tempo and timing. I like to think of tempo as the overall rhythm of the swing. What is important about it is that it be natural for you. Gene Littler and my hero, Sam Snead, had wonderfully graceful tempos. But Ben Hogan and guys from today's tour, like Lanny Wadkins and Greg Norman, are much faster. There is no right or wrong to this unless you're trying to do something unnatural for yourself. My tempo is rather slow and unhurried but it's not Larry Mize's ultra long slow motion. As has been said before, "There's only room for one fast motion in the swing." Let that occur as close to impact as possible.

SECRET NO. 47: KEEP IT SIMPLE.

Timing has much more to do with the sequence of things during the swing. It is in this area that most of the compensations for bad balance, position, or motion are revealed. If the club has gotten into a poor position from which to begin the downswing, the hands will have to compensate in order to get the clubface squared "in time." By concentrating on getting things working in the right order, we can avoid some of these complications. On the downswing, it's feet, legs, hips, shoulders, arms, hands and club . . .ever so slightly following one another. "Lateness is Greatness" is the essence of the sequential lagging which must take place to achieve good timing in the swing. By practicing good timing, the mechanical positions of your swing will naturally work themselves into better shape.

My last word on this subject is build a repeatable swing and then try to improve it little by little over time.

SECRET No. 32

TRUST YOUR CLUB SELECTION

If you've judged the distance properly and you know your capabilities through all your practice, you should *know* you've got the right club for the job. You should have no indecision whatsoever, and be ready to make a smooth, natural swing.

DON'T UNDERCLUB

Always give yourself enough club. Don't try to hit a 3 iron from the rough when a 4 wood would do the job a lot easier. On a long par 3, don't go up there with an iron in your hand when you should be using a wood. They use the term in putting, but it works just as well for any golf shot . . . "Never up, never in."

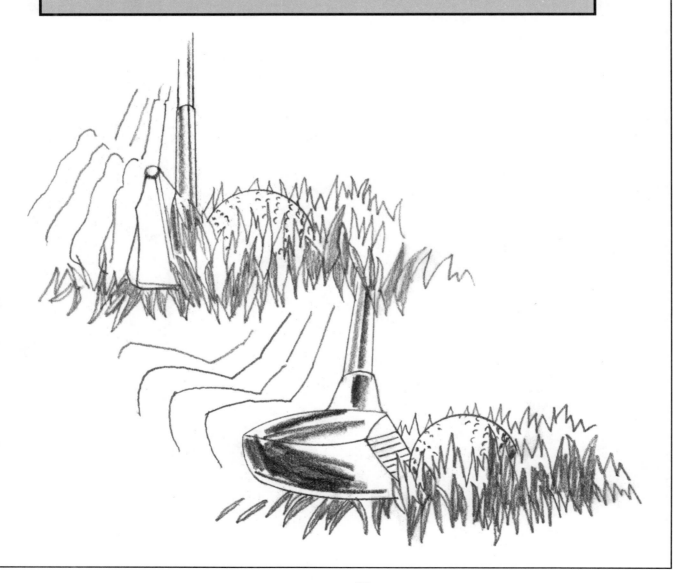

GET A GRIP —
AND STAY WITH IT

The importance of gripping the club properly is something that is constantly overlooked by the average golfer. There are three generally accepted grips — the Vardon, or overlapping grip, is used by most. Then there is the interlocking grip, and the ten fingered, or baseball grip. Use the one that is most comfortable to you.

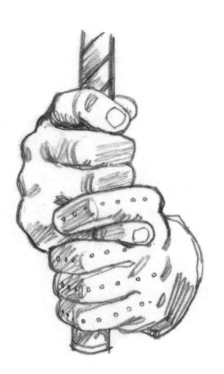  

LOSE CONTROL
TO GAIN CONTROL

The biggest problem the average golfer has with the grip is squeezing it too tight. Loosen up — and you should be able to get a feel for the hands working "as one" throughout the swing. You want to be feeling the weight of the clubhead rather than the pressure of the grip.

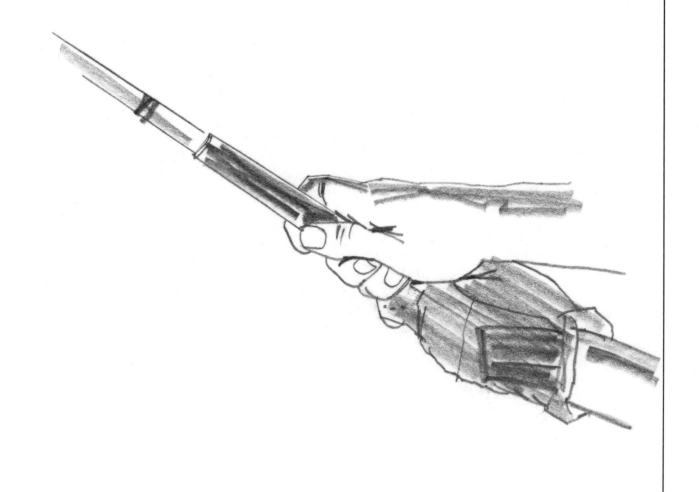

SECRET No. 36

ADDRESS THE BALL NATURALLY

Begin by getting a good grip with your hands out directly in front of your face at about arm's length. Then, with your knees flexed and at the proper width, allow your arms to drop slowly. As your elbows make contact with your body, allow your upper body to bend into a natural, relaxed posture. When the clubhead makes contact with the ground, you're there.

PLACE THE BALL IN THE RIGHT POSITION

Here's a simple way to approach ball position: always play the ball off the inside of your left heel. Start with a wider stance with the driver, and then move your right foot closer in as the clubs get shorter. This will adjust your center of gravity just enough to positively affect the arc of your swing through the ball.

SECRET No. 38

FIRST THE TARGET —
THEN THE BALL

Use this two-step approach to proper alignment. First, closely align the clubface to the target. Then, keeping your attention down at the ball, you can square your stance in relation to the ball and clubhead — knowing that you are already lined up properly with the target. You can swing away, knowing that you're positioned properly.

ONE PIECE, ONE MOVING PART

Think of the dynamics of your backswing as a single sequence instead of a series of parts. You will be miles ahead. Though in reality there is a slight lag between the initial motion of the club, hands, arms, shoulders, hips, and legs, you are better off thinking of your backswing as a "one piece take-away" and letting it all happen naturally.

73

SECRET No. 40

LET THE
LARGE MUSCLES LEAD

You want your big muscles to control the movement of the club as you coil in the backswing. Put your hips and shoulders into it — not the hands and arms. You should feel a natural transference of weight to the inside of the right knee.

DON'T HINGE ... COCK!

Be aware that your wrists should not hinge from side to side during any part of the swing. Keep your wrists firm without tightening up on the grip. This allows the momentum of the club to come into play without "throwing it from the top" or sending the club off line by over-controlling it.

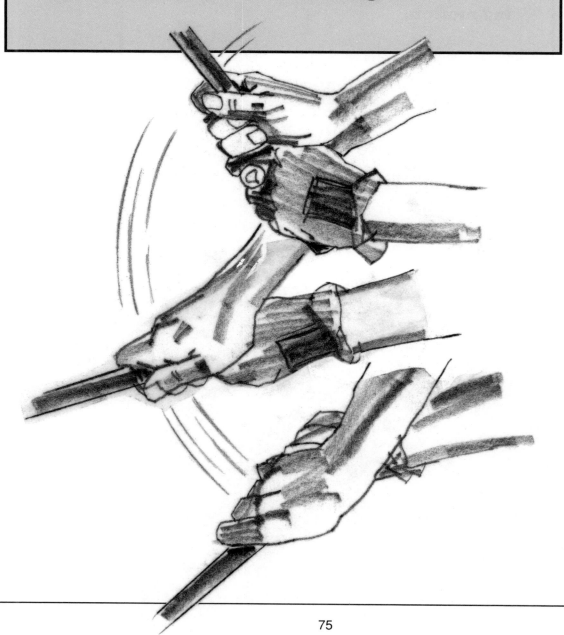

YOUR LOWER BODY
TRIGGERS THE DOWNSWING

In triggering the downswing, again think of the large muscles of the body rather than just the arms and hands. At the same moment the upper body has completed its coil, the lower body should already be triggered into a forward and left turning motion.

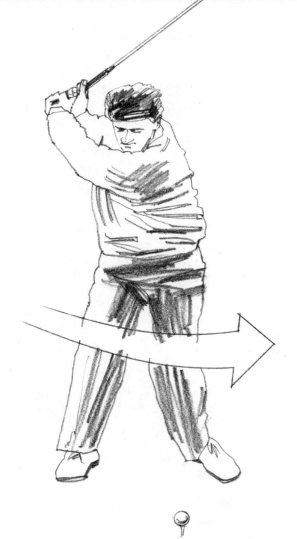

GO LEFT, YOUNG MAN, *LEFT*

Turn your left hip *left* — not toward the target — as you move into the downswing. You don't want too much of a lateral slide, you want a *turn*. Don't be afraid to exaggerate as you practice this turning motion. In fact, the right hip will actually end up closer to the target than the left hip at the full follow through position!

SECRET No. 44

EXTEND "THROUGH" THE BALL

The bottom line for a full swing is to create a complete, circular swinging motion. Don't think about hitting "at" the ball. Think of the full swing as the coiling and uncoiling of the body — using the large muscles. The arms, wrists, and hands should remain relaxed and reactive to the turning motion rather than taking on independent activities of their own.

BALANCE YOUR SWING

Maintaining good balance is an important key throughout the golf swing. If you tend to lose balance out over your toes, your shots will go left. If you tend to lose balance falling back, your shots will go right. Your weight shift needs to be moving back in your backswing, and forward — through the ball — in your downswing.

SECRET No. 46

FIND YOUR OWN TEMPO

Think about tempo as the overall rhythm of the swing. It's most important that you find your own rhythm — and go with it. There is no right or wrong tempo unless you are trying to do something that is unnatural for yourself.

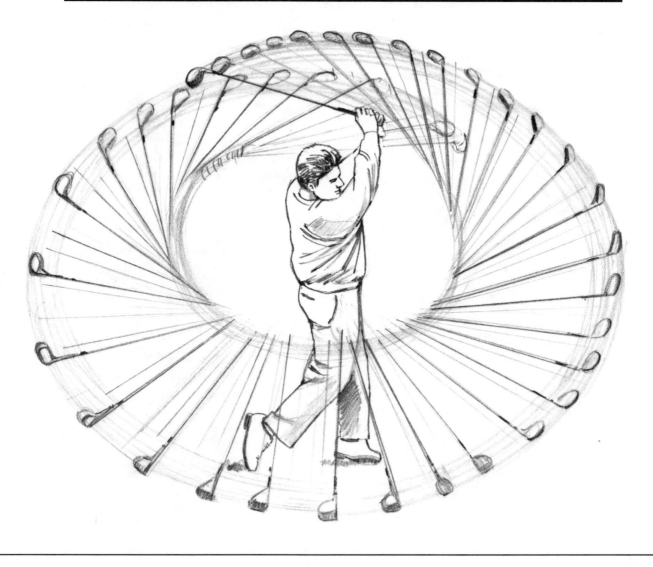

KEEP IT SIMPLE

By concentrating on simply getting things working in the right order during the swing, we can avoid the mental complications that result in a major breakdown. On the downswing, it's feet, legs, hips, shoulders, arms, hands, and club ... ever so slightly following one another *through* the ball.

Part

6

The Secrets of Overcoming the Seven Deadly Sins

6

As a golf director, I see some of the same mistakes over and over again. I call them the "Seven Deadly Sins of Golf." If you are cursed with one or several, you'll notice your golf score rising right along with your blood pressure.

The good news is that the "Seven Deadly Sins of Golf" have seven easy solutions. All it takes is a little patience and a little practice.

SECRET NO. 48: DON'T CHOKE IT TO DEATH.

Imagine that you're a professional golfer and you're coming to me moaning about your game. The first thing I'll say to you is, "Let me see your grip."

After all, the only thing touching the club are your hands so obviously it's important. The fact is, if you start out in a poor position with your hands, the ball will end up in a poor position.

Your hands should be placed on the club naturally, gently, and comfortably. Your left and right hand should complement and face one another. The V's formed by the index finger and thumb on each hand should be pointing at the inside of the right shoulder.

Keep your hands close together. The closer they feel, the more your two hands will act as a single unit.

Most golfers think they need to grip the club hard in order to hit it hard.

Just the opposite.

A tense muscle is a slow muscle and clubhead speed is the primary distance factor. Grip it lightly and keep it light throughout the swing. In practice only, be conscious of your grip pressure throughout the swing. A constant light touch is ideal.

I like to think of it as if you're holding a bird in your hand. You don't want to hold it too lightly, or it will get loose and fly away—but you also want to make sure that you hold it light enough to avoid crushing it within your grasp.

SECRET NO. 49: DON'T SET UP TOO FAR FROM THE BALL.

One thing every professional golfer knows: your eyes deceive you. You will figure out a way to hit the ball, regardless of its position. A lot of average to good players work themselves too far away from the ball over time. They also start playing the ball too far forward in their stance.

Be sure you're not reaching for the ball with your hands, and that you're not letting your weight get in front of the balls of your feet. You should be able to wiggle your toes inside your shoes. Sam Snead taught me this and, of course, early in Sam's career, he played some golf with no shoes at all. So I consider The Slammer a real authority on the toes.

Here's a good way to find the perfect ball position:

Flex your knees and get into your best stance, but hold the club up in the air out in front of you. Close your eyes and just let your arms and the club drop gently. It will seek

6

its own position and show you how far you should be away from the ball. If you try this without closing your eyes, you will tend to drop the club where you think it should be.

SECRET NO. 50: DON'T LINE UP TO THE RIGHT.

Perfect alignment is certainly something to work toward, but one of the most common mistakes I see is players inadvertently aiming too far to the right of their target.

Use the Nicklaus system of alignment to an intermediate target as described in Secret No. 38. Then be sure you are lined up parallel to the target line, not at the target.

If you line up at or slightly to the right of the target, the left side of your body cuts off your swing as you try to get through the ball. So don't line up right. Line up correctly. Line up left of your target.

How much depends on the distance to the target. As you look down a railroad track, the tracks seem to come together in the distance, don't they? You must actually line up slightly open or left to be right. Clear?

SECRET NO. 51: DON'T WORRY ABOUT MOVING YOUR HEAD.

Poorer players shift their weight to the right side on the backswing and leave it there on the downswing. The poorest players, though, don't shift their weight at all — right or left. They don't move because they're trying to keep their head still.

You really must allow yourself a little lateral movement on the backswing in order to transfer your weight to the right side. Let the weight go in the direction the club is moving.

When you begin your downswing and the turning of your left side out of the way, the weight must transfer to the left side. This is the direction the club is going. All the great players make this move. Trevino is great, Faldo, Strange. You really can't play this game well if you can't get this move down.

SECRET NO. 52: DON'T HIT "AT" THE BALL.

A lot of golfers become ball bound. They over-control their swing because they're so conscious of striking the ball.

But if you think about hitting *through* the ball and not at it, you'll add distance every time. You'll hit the ball more solidly, harder, and with much less effort.

Lee Trevino said, "Don't anticipate the hit." Tommy Aaron said, "Sneak up on the ball with your practice swing." But no matter how you say it, when a golfer is "in the groove," he's getting all the way to the finish because he's striking through the ball and not at it.

Here's a good way to solve your problem if you've become overly conscious of striking the ball: practice hitting leaves, or whiffle golf balls, or golf balls into a net. The less thought you have about the ball, ball flight, or any possible consequences of the swing, the more natural and fluid your swing will be.

SECRET NO. 53: DON'T BE TOO ANALYTICAL.

Most golfers try to hit the perfect shot every time and that holds them back.

Just like the ball bound golfer above, they over-control the club. They get too tense. And tense muscles don't do what they're supposed to do.

Relax. Don't get so caught up in your swing keys, your partner's advice, or the latest issue you read in *Golf Digest* that you suffer from "paralysis by analysis."

Remember, if you've prepared yourself properly and gotten to a point where you can "groove" your swing, you should only be thinking about one or two keys at the most when you swing. "Let it happen." Don't try to "make it happen." When he's doing it right, a good golfer can swing with his eyes closed ... which is not a bad drill to try on the range from time to time.

SECRET NO. 54: DON'T WORRY ... BE HAPPY!

Golf is a reflection of what's going on in your life. If your wife is mad at you, your kids are acting up, and work isn't going well, it will show up in your golf game.

You can't change everything in your life but you can put yourself in the mood to play your best golf. Take your time. Don't rush around. Slow yourself down a bit.

Drive to the course slowly and be sure you get there in plenty of time before you have to tee off. Establish a controlled warm-up routine at the course. Go to the practice tee. Spend some time on the putting green. Get yourself in the right motion, the right tone, and the right tempo for your round.

Golf is as much a game of self control as it is a game of skill. You're there to shake off the rest of the day and have a good time. So relax and have fun.

DON'T CHOKE IT TO DEATH

Most golfers think they have to grip the club hard to hit it hard. Actually it's just the opposite. A tense muscle is a slow muscle. And clubhead speed is the primary distance factor. So grip it lightly and keep it light throughout the swing.

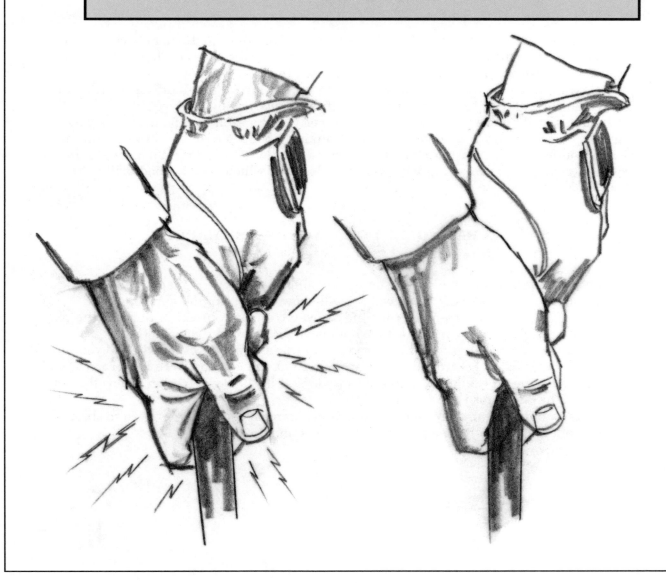

DON'T SET UP TOO FAR
FROM THE BALL

A lot of average to good golfers work themselves too far away from the ball over time. Be sure that you're not reaching for the ball, and that you're not letting your weight get in front of the balls of your feet. Take a tip Sam Snead taught me and be sure that you're able to wiggle your toes inside your shoes.

SECRET No. 50

DON'T LINE UP TO THE RIGHT

Many golfers make the mistake of lining up too far to the right of their target. If you do, the left side of your body cuts off your swing as you try to get through the ball. You should actually be lining up slightly left of your target with your body, shoulders, and feet—but paralleling the target line.

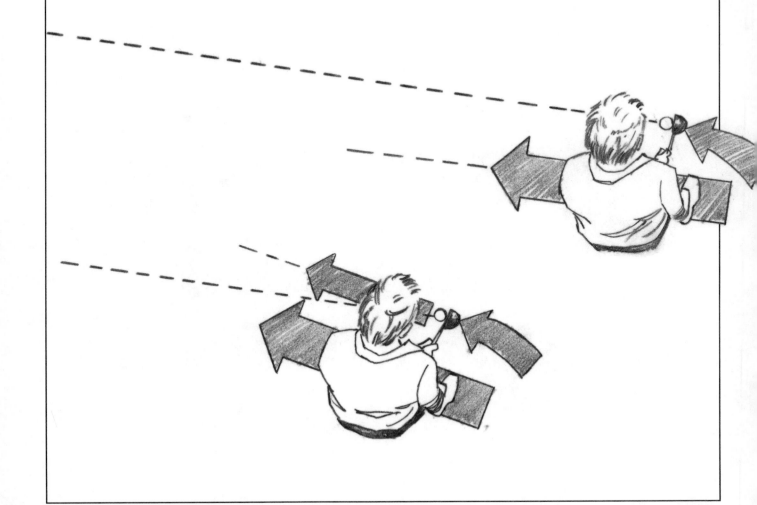

DON'T WORRY ABOUT MOVING YOUR HEAD

Poor players shift their weight to the right side on the backswing and then leave it there on the downswing. The poorest players don't shift their weight at all because they're too worried about moving their head. Allow yourself a little lateral movement to properly transfer your weight. Let the weight go in the direction the club is moving.

SECRET No. 52

DON'T HIT "AT" THE BALL

A lot of golfers become ball bound. They over-control their swing because they're so conscious of striking the ball properly. If you think about hitting "through" the ball rather than "at" it, you'll hit it more solidly, harder, and with much less effort.

DON'T BE TOO ANALYTICAL

Most golfers try to hit the perfect shot every time, and that holds them back. They're suffering from "paralysis by analysis." Always remember, if you've prepared yourself properly, and "grooved" your swing, you will be in position to "let it happen" rather than "make it happen."

SECRET No. 54

DON'T WORRY ... BE HAPPY!

Golf is a reflection of what's going on in your life. You can't play your best game if you're too busy rushing to the first tee, or thinking about all the minor crises going on at home or at the office. Relax. Take your time. You're there to shake off the rest of the day and have a good time.

Part

7

The Secrets of Wood Play

7

ow that we've got the basics of the game covered, it's time to get into some of the specifics. I'll take you right down the fairway, starting with the secrets of "wood play" ...

Wood clubs, regardless of the material from which they are made, are all made to serve a common purpose. They are primarily distance clubs. The driver is designed to give us maximum distance. In the chapter on equipment I discussed some of the design and material differences available today. Metal heads are usually built with lower centers of gravity, although some manufacturers are beginning to move the weight off the sole now and get it a little higher in the head. This will lower the trajectory of the ball flight somewhat.

Wood clubs, in the generic sense, are different than irons for certain other reasons. For instance, you should use the top edge of a wood club to align the face of the club.

The faces of wood clubs are almost never flat surfaces. They are designed with bulge and roll. The bulge of a clubface is its curvature from heel to toe across the face. The roll is the curvature from top to bottom across the face. Without going overboard on the technical stuff, let me just say that bulge in particular can really affect the shape of your shots in bringing a mishit shot back on line. If you are really interested in equipment you might be interested in learning more about bulge, roll, face progression, and some of the more technical aspects of wood or metal clubs.

SECRET NO. 55: AIM LEFT OF TARGET.

For the time being, let's make use of the driver you've got. As I mentioned earlier, you've got to aim or align your body a little left of the target in order to be correctly aligned. On the drive this is critical because your target is down the fairway over 200 yards away. Aim your shoulders about 10 or 15 yards to the left of your target. If you are lined up too far right, each time you look up to sight your target your brain is going to be getting this signal that the target is left of your alignment. Before long your body will begin to adjust and you will be pulling across your body on every drive in an unconscious attempt to get the ball on target. Your good swing will get cut off by your left side and your shots at the target will all be pulls.

SECRET NO. 56: TEE HIGH FOR DISTANCE, LOW FOR ACCURACY.

"Tee it high and let it fly!" I've heard that all my life and it's true. The year I won The Colonial NIT in Fort Worth, Texas, I put this little reminder to good use. The third hole at Colonial Country Club is a very long par 4, dogleg to the left. At the corner of the

7

dogleg are some huge oak trees. If you could get a ball past those trees you could gain about 50 yards on the hole. Each of the four days on that hole I teed my ball on my pencil rather than on a regular tee and blew it over those trees.

By the same token, when I am more interested in accuracy out of a tee shot or naturally if there is wind in my face or strong cross winds, I will tee it lower. Be careful with this, though, because you must avoid letting a lower tee position affect your swing. If you've got wind against you, you don't want to be hitting down on the ball at a steep angle.

SECRET NO. 57: SLOW EVERYTHING DOWN FOR MORE POWER.

To get maximum distance from your drives, you should learn to slow yourself down in the early part of the swing. Pay particular attention on getting the bigger muscles of the body involved in the backswing. Secondly, keep your grip and arm muscles as loose and relaxed as you can. Thirdly, don't anticipate impact. Swing "through" it.

Your own experience will tell you that your most solid impacts send the ball the farthest. When you're trying to really let out on one, make sure you hit it SOLID!

SECRET NO. 58: HIT DOWN ON IT.

I guess Fred Couples finding a magic 3 wood in Tom Watson's garage is a recent example of what fairway woods have meant to the better players. I know Lee has made a lot of money with a 6 wood he carries from time to time, and Raymond Floyd credited a Masters victory to his use of a 5 wood one year. There is no doubt, these clubs are valuable. Maybe more valuable in the average player's bag than ours.

The setup adjustment for fairway woods is small. The right foot should be a little closer to the left than for the Driver. This moves your center of gravity a little more over the ball and encourages a bit more "down" angle into the back of the ball. Deane Beaman was one of the best fairway wood players I played with and he always took a little divot with these clubs. He didn't really try to sweep them. He hit down on them and let the loft of the club get it in the air.

SECRET NO. 59: DON'T HIT A 3 WOOD IN MOISTURE.

If the turf is wet from early morning dew or from rain or something, I would avoid the 3 wood out of the grass. Now, with the metal woods — which I highly recommend for fairway woods — it's a little easier. But always remember, moisture decreases the backspin imparted to the ball and makes it much harder to get the ball in the air. Under these conditions it would be better to use a 4 or 5 wood for the same shot.

SECRET NO. 60: USE A METAL WOOD WITH A WEAK SHAFT.

In a similar vein, I think most players should use a little weaker shaft in their fairway woods, or at least one with a lower kick point. These factors help get the ball in the air a little faster. And since you don't always draw a perfect lie, even in the fairway, a metal wood will cut through the grass much better than a "wood" wood.

Believe me, if you're having trouble getting the ball up in the air with a fairway wood, a "metal" wood with a certain degree of flexibility could be all you need!

SECRET NO. 61: THERE SHOULD BE A 5 WOOD IN EVERY BAG.

If you are not a particularly long hitter, the fairway woods are clubs you want to get to know on a first name basis. Deane Beaman became an excellent fairway wood player because he lacked the length off the tee compared to some of the other guys. But as I've been saying, you must learn your strengths and weaknesses; play to your strengths and develop your own game.

You may play with guys who insist on pulling out a 2 iron on 200 yard par 3's when everyone in the group, including the guy hitting, knows he doesn't have a prayer of getting it to the green with that club. More often than not, there's kind of an ego thing involved. If you pull out a 5 wood on a long par 3 hole, everyone is going to question your manhood. Now I don't think there's anything manly about taking a 9 on a par 3 because you put two in the water, and then started seeing the wheels come off. It's up to you, but I admire an accurate wood player.

SECRET No. 55

AIM LEFT OF TARGET

Align your body a little left of target for a drive 200 yards down the fairway; your shoulders should be aimed 10 to 15 yards to the left of the target. If you are lined up too far to the right, you'll end up pulling across your body from the outside in.

TEE HIGH FOR DISTANCE, LOW FOR ACCURACY

If you're looking for distance on your shot, tee the ball higher. If you're interested in accuracy — or if you're faced with strong winds — tee the ball lower. When you do this, however, be sure you don't hit down on the ball at a steeper angle.

SECRET No. 57

SLOW EVERYTHING DOWN FOR MORE POWER

Slowing yourself down in the early part of your swing will get you the maximum distance in your drives. Be sure to get your bigger muscles involved in the backswing, keep your grip and arm muscles as relaxed as possible and don't anticipate the impact. Swing "through" it and hit the ball solid.

HIT DOWN ON IT

When using a fairway wood, your right foot should be placed a little closer to the left foot than for the driver. This encourages a little more "down" angle into the back of the ball. Hit down and let the loft of the club get the ball in the air.

SECRET No. 59

DON'T HIT A 3 WOOD IN MOISTURE

If the turf is wet, avoid using a 3 wood out of the grass. If you're using a metal wood, it's a little easier. But moisture decreases the ball's backspin and makes it harder to get the ball in the air. It's better to use a 4 or 5 wood for the shot.

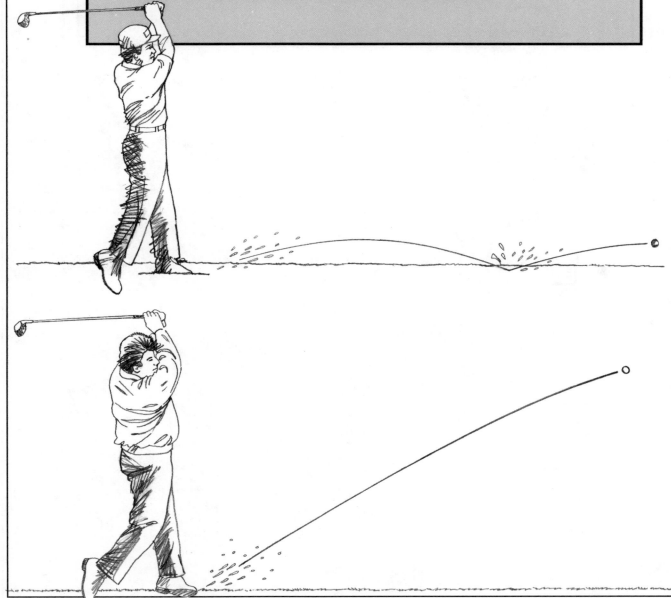

SECRET No. 60

USE A METAL WOOD
WITH A WEAK SHAFT

If you're having trouble getting loft on the ball with a fairway wood, a metal wood with a degree of flexibility is the answer. A metal wood with a weaker shaft, and/or a lower kick point, will help get the ball in the air faster.

SECRET No. 61

THERE SHOULD BE A 5 WOOD IN EVERY BAG

Be honest with yourself. If you don't hit the long irons very well or with confidence, why are you still using a 2 iron on long par 3's? Because everyone else does? Play to your strengths. Switch to a 5 wood on a long par 3 hole and become an accurate wood player. Your scorecard will reflect the change.

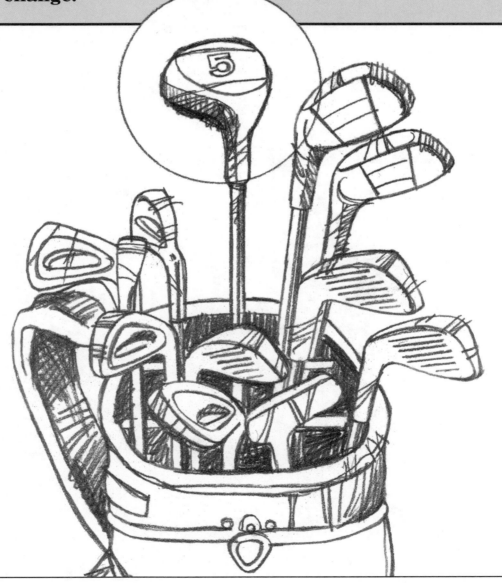

Part

8

The Secrets of Long and Middle Iron Play

Now that we've got the Woods covered, it's time to get into "Iron" play. In this part, I'll be talking about how the pros look at playing longer irons, and then say a few words about the middle-range irons as well ...

SECRET NO. 62: IN ROUGH, BETTER TO USE A FAIRWAY WOOD.

The first thing to know about long irons is when to use them and when not to. Don't try to hit long irons from bad lies in general. A 1 iron has almost the exact same loft as a 3 wood and it's shorter than a 3 wood. In almost every case, though, I would say the fairway woods will be easier to hit from marginal to bad lies.

The reason is the design of the clubhead. When you try to play a long iron out of deep grass, the grass can, and usually does, wrap around the hossel of the iron as the club-head approaches the ball. This closes the clubface, taking loft out of it, and prevents you from getting the ball airborne and out of the rough. When you swing a fairway wood through the same grass, the depth of the clubhead minimizes most of this closing tendency, and the clubface remains in its normal lofted position when it contacts the ball.

SECRET NO. 63: A LONG AND SLOW GOLF SWING.

The best long iron players from my days on tour were Nicklaus and Weiskopf. They were better than most, not because of their strength so much, but because of the length of their swings. To play really good long irons it helps to have a long swing. Out of today's tour players I think Payne Stewart is an example of this. Davis Love and Fred Couples are good examples, too.

Of course, you will want to adjust your stance by moving your right foot just a little closer to your left for these clubs. It is also important to try and get your shoulders as parallel to the slope of the ground as you can. This is true with all of the longer clubs, from fairway woods down through the 5 iron. If you're on sloping ground, try to stand more or less perpendicular to it so that your shoulders will be pretty level.

The swing technique to practice with these clubs is kind of a Catch 22 problem. In order to make the best golf swings with the long irons, you must believe you can hit them well. The sheer anxiety that most average players experience prior to and during their long iron shots is the very thing that prevents them from hitting them well. Either they don't complete the backswing or they get so tense and bound up at the top of the backswing that they jump at it from the top.

If you use early hands in a long iron swing you have no chance of hitting a good shot. Lateness is greatness with these clubs. Think about the swing, not the impact. You may

8

have heard or read that these clubs should be "swept" rather than swung down and through the ball. The danger in that advice, to me, is that most players who attempt a more sweeping motion actually lift up on the swing. I just don't think any shot can be made very well by trying to help it get in the air. Stay down and through it, and take a small shallow divot just like the fairway woods are played. Passive hands and a long steady swing with no fast moves will have you hitting these clubs better. And a little success will eliminate the fear.

SECRET NO. 64: CONSIDER THE COURSE AND CONDITIONS.

In selecting which clubs ought to be in your golf bag for the course you play the most, keep in mind the characteristics of the course and the shot each alternative club produces. Long irons tend to produce a lower trajectory ball flight than the comparable fairway wood. If your course has fairly hard fairways and/or nice entries to the greens, the long irons might be the best answer. If your course is on the soft side where you won't get much roll, carrying the ball in the air a little farther with a 4 or 5 wood might be smarter. Elevated greens or greens protected by water hazards and deep bunkers in front would discourage me from trying to fit too many low screamers in there.

That brings us to the other important consideration, which is wind. As you know, the fairway woods will tend to fly a little higher, so if you live in West Texas or Florida or anywhere the wind stays pretty strong, I would suggest you really spend some time working on becoming a better long iron player.

SECRET NO. 65: MIDDLE IRONS — SET UP FOR SUCCESS.

I'm an advocate of playing this game in its simplest form, so I certainly don't want to suggest that you try to make a different swing with each club. By taking your time on your setup and especially on your alignment, there's no reason you shouldn't expect good results out of the middle irons. Just as before, of course, you will be setting your right foot a bit closer to the left as your clubs get shorter.

Sam Snead was a wonderful middle-iron player, as was my good friend Johnny Miller. Their tempo was so good. When you think of the swings of a guy like Gene Littler, you just think of fluid tempo, a kind of unhurried acceleration.

What some people do when they try to copy a swing like Sam's is they get lazy instead of smooth. All of these guys are ultra smooth but their swings are not lazy.

SECRET NO. 66: GO FOR THE GREEN!

When you practice with these clubs, think about how and where you use them on the golf course. The 4, 5 and 6 irons are often used for approach shots on par 4 holes and as tee shots on par 3's. Your goal or expectation for these clubs should be to put the ball on the green most of the time. Now, that might give you around a 15- to 20-yard margin of error. Be sure to practice some shots using a tee. The ball feels and acts differently from a tee, so get used to it. This is an important scoring shot. Work toward establishing a shot pattern within these parameters by paying close attention to your alignment, ball position and balance. Don't make the mistake of over-swinging with a 6 iron, when you could have made a normal swing effort with a 5 iron in your hand. By the same token, don't decelerate and quit on a 4 iron, when you could have gone to the 5. For the real "in between" distances on any club, choke down rather than let up.

SECRET No. 62

IN ROUGH, BETTER TO USE A FAIRWAY WOOD

When you've got a marginal to bad lie, reach for a fairway wood, not a long iron. When you swing a fairway wood through deep grass, the clubface remains in a lofted position when it makes contact with the ball. A long iron tends to get tied up in the grass, causing the clubface to close.

A LONG AND SLOW
GOLF SWING

In order to make the best swings with the long irons, you must believe you can hit them well. So, relax. Think about the swing, not the impact. Lateness is greatness with long irons. Passive hands and a long steady swing are the keys to success.

SECRET No. 64

CONSIDER THE COURSE AND CONDITIONS

If the course has fairly hard fairways and/or nice entries to the greens, long irons should work well. If the course is on the soft side where you won't get much roll, a 4 or 5 wood will help carry the ball in the air farther. If the course has elevated greens or greens protected by water hazards, come prepared to avoid low screamers.

SECRET No. 65

MIDDLE IRONS —
SETUP FOR SUCCESS

Take your time on your setup and alignment. Set your right foot a bit closer to your left as your clubs get shorter. Your swing should be fluid, a kind of unhurried acceleration. But, you don't want a lazy swing. You want an ultra smooth swing.

SECRET No. 66

GO FOR THE GREEN

The 4, 5 and 6 irons are often used for approach shots on par 4's and tee shots on par 3's. The goal is to put the ball on the green most of the time. Establish a shot pattern within these parameters. Don't over-swing with a 6 iron when a 5 iron will do; don't decelerate with a 4 iron when you could have used a 5 iron.

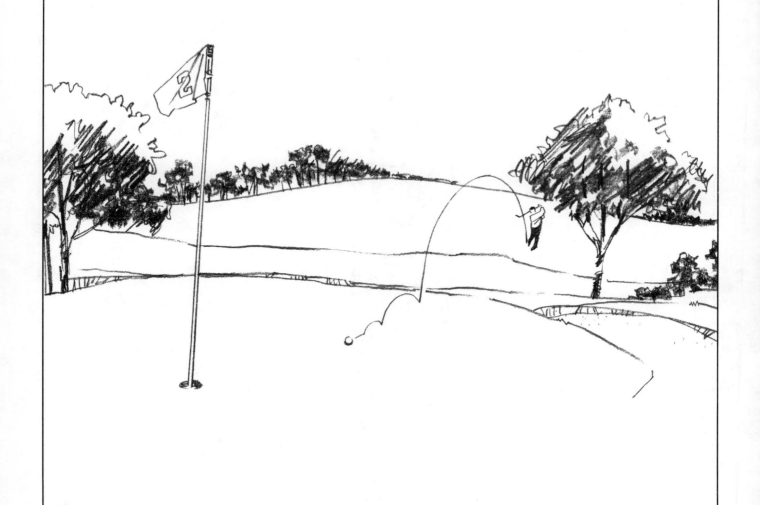

Part

9

The Secrets of Short Iron Play

9

Now we're getting down to the part of the game that can really make a difference on the scorecard. The longest hitter in the world won't win unless he has a good short game. Here are some secrets from the pros' perspective ...

SECRET NO. 67: DON'T "SCOOP" — USE A NATURAL SWING.

When I see the average player playing a full short iron shot, I see a kind of scooping action at the ball. Because the trajectory of the shot is higher and shorter than with other clubs, I guess they think they need to help the ball up in the air by lifting. No sooner than the club starts its downswing, you'll see this kind of player lift up with some part of the body. It may be his left shoulder or the straightening of the knees, but as a reaction to the downward effort, something is coming up.

Of course, you know better. You know you should swing down and through the shots, right? The first adjustment you make for the 7, 8, 9 and pitching wedge shots is to narrow up the stance a little by moving the right foot in. By now, with each successive move of the right foot, the ball will be pretty close to the middle of your stance. That's enough of an adjustment that you really don't need to try to go at it more steeply, or reduce your swing radius by trying to scoop the ball with your arms and hands.

To a large degree, the more out and the less up these shots begin, the better you're going to like the result.

SECRET NO. 68: "TRAP" THE BALL TO THE HOLE.

The best short iron players over the years, guys like Trevino, Casper, and a lot of people put me in that group, have one thing in common. We try to draw, or "trap," our short irons. Now Billy turns *everything* over so that's not news, but Lee is rather noted for cutting his ball from left to right. Not with his short irons though, and through the years of televised golf, I'm surprised this doesn't get mentioned.

The drawn short iron shot doesn't have a lot of curvature to it because it's not a very long shot and with the loft of an 8, 9 or pitching wedge, it is difficult to move it very far from right to left.

Think of trapping the ball between the clubface and the ground. The best results will come if you are swinging the clubhead from inside the target line and the toe of the clubface is passing the heel at the moment of impact. To accomplish this, you will need to add a little emphasis to the release of the club through the ball. Relax your hands and wrists, and get a mental image of the toe passing the heel and you'll do it.

Since the toe of the clubface prevents the ball from starting out too much to the right, the clubhead path from the inside of the target line is trying to make it start right, and the ground is not going anywhere but the clubhead is coming down and through the ball, the ball is trapped. But you really can't get the best result out of this shot if your swing is kind of long and lazy. This is going to be a lower flying, penetrating trajectory. What you don't want is a floater. A ball flying up there at the full mercy of the wind.

In order to get the most out of this shot, you want to reduce the length of your backswing down to maybe 3/4 of its normal length. Then you also want to go at the ball with a firmer, more aggressive move — a sharper, more authoritative swing. Don't make this move with your hands and arms. That's where the scoop comes from. You will get a shallower, more positive move if the large muscles of the body are in control. The sharper release of the club to get the toe past the heel should come from the body turning left, not from the hands taking control of the club. As you swing your arms through the hitting area, the closer they are to your body, more of your body will be in your shots. These short iron shots in particular will benefit from that kind of move.

SECRET NO. 69: GO FOR THE PIN!

The short irons are most definitely considered scoring clubs. When you have these clubs in your hands you hope you are in position to be knocking some pins down. As mentioned before, be smart. You shouldn't try to shoot at "sucker" pin positions. On the other hand, you'd like to get good enough with the short irons so that it will be tough to hide any pins from you. Particularly with the pitching wedge in your hand, you want to practice until you can get that into a 10-yard diameter circle. That would mean you should expect no more than a 15-foot putt thereafter. Don't be discouraged if you're not anywhere close to that now. It's a goal for you to work toward with these clubs.

SECRET NO. 70: WATCH FOR A "FLYER."

A word about "lies." The lie of the golf ball always determines what is possible. In other words, a given situation may call for putting a lot of spin on a ball in order to stick it in tight on the hole. If you've got grass immediately behind the ball, you're not going to spin it, nor am I. Recognize what different lies will allow you to do and what kind of shots are eliminated. This goes back to playing the higher percentage shot.

If, as in the case above, you've got some grass against the back of the ball, you should be aware of the possibility of hitting a "flyer." A flyer is a ball with very little backspin. When the club and ball normally make contact, the angle of the clubface and the angle of the approach of the clubhead act on the ball in such a way as to impart backspin to the ball. When grass gets in between the surface of the ball and the clubface, the backspin is reduced tremendously. A flyer results and it means an out-of-control ball flight. Sometimes they will literally fly an extra 10, 15 or 20 yards, and sometimes they will dive back to ground prematurely and roll a mile.

When you find yourself with one of these flyer lies, my best advice is to try and give yourself some extra margin for error. This is not the time to go for the tight pin placements. If you can shoot for the fat part of the green, do so. Try to find a line which will accommodate a short or long shot without getting in too much trouble.

SECRET NO. 71: FOR BACKSPIN, CONSIDER THE CONDITIONS.

Speaking of spin, let's discuss backspin just for a bit. One of the primary reasons you see tour players spinning the ball to such a great degree on television is the condition of the golf courses we play on. It takes virtually perfect conditions on both ends of the shot to really pull the string on a shot.

First and foremost, to put spin to the ball you need a dry ball and clubface for friction to be at its greatest. As mentioned, no grass or other foreign material can get between those surfaces. And the fairways on your golf course are probably not mowed as tightly as those we play on week in and week out. The next very important factor is the type of golf ball being used. If you're not using a soft balata cover ball, it will be extremely difficult to get much spin going. Lastly, the surface of the clubface is an important factor. I carry a third wedge in my bag most of the time that has a virtually smooth face, no grooves at all. I use it to *avoid* spinning the ball.

Once you get the ball spinning, it has to have some other conditions in its favor to actually back up on the surface of the green. If you are playing the shot downwind, it is going to be difficult to pull it back. If the surface of the green is particularly hard the action will be reduced. Think of the way you've seen balls react to U.S. Open greens versus a normal tour stop venue. If the surface of the green is sloping away from you like on the back side of a bunker or a steep contour of the green itself, the backspin on the ball will never have a chance to stop the ball.

So there you go. You must have ideal conditions to spin the ball. Still, some guys spin it much more so than others. Greg Norman spins it more than just about anybody. Maybe too much. Spinning the ball can get you into trouble as well as working in your favor. It looks good, but it's not always the right shot to play. Picking and choosing when and how to spin the ball is a fine tuning to your game that can really help your score.

SECRET No. 67

DON'T "SCOOP" —
USE A NATURAL SWING

Always swing down and through shots when you use short irons. Don't "scoop" the ball. For 7, 8, 9 irons and pitching wedge shots, narrow up your stance by moving your right foot in. As you do so, the ball will be close to the middle of your stance.

"TRAP" THE BALL TO THE HOLE

To get the most out of a short iron shot, swing the clubhead from inside the target line with the toe of the clubface passing the head at the moment of impact. Relax your hands and wrists. Reduce the length of your backswing to 3/4 or 1/2 of its normal length. You want a sharp, authoritative swing with your large muscles in control.

SECRET No. 69

GO FOR THE PIN

Since the short irons are considered scoring clubs, you should knock some pins down with these clubs. Practice with the pitching wedge until you get within a 10-yard diameter circle. Then you can expect no more than a 15-foot putt thereafter. You may not be there now, but practice will close the gap.

WATCH FOR THE "FLYER"

When grass gets between the surface of the ball and the clubface, you're stuck with a "flyer," which is a ball with little backspin. The result is often out-of-control ball flight. Allow yourself some margin for error. Don't go for tight pin placements. Find a line that will accommodate a short or long shot, preferably to the fat part of the green.

SECRET No. 71

FOR BACKSPIN, CONSIDER THE CONDITIONS

To create spin, you need a dry ball and clubface. No grass or foreign material can get between those surfaces. Use a soft balata cover ball and a clean clubface. And consider that you need ideal conditions to create backspin. So pick and choose carefully.

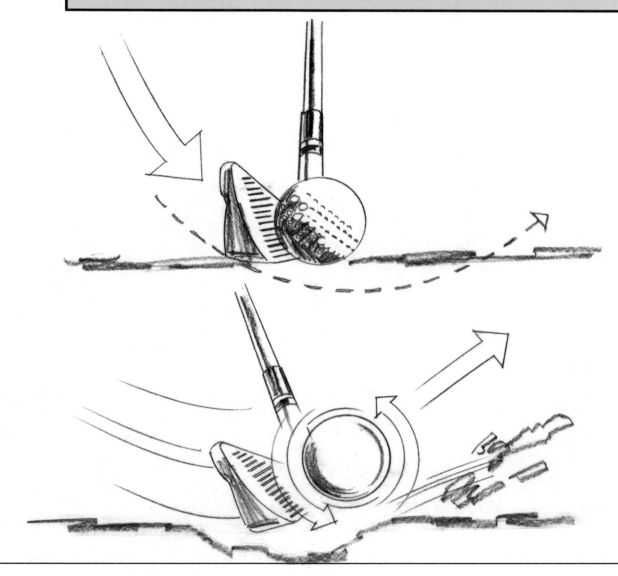

Part

10

The Secrets of
Chipping & Sand Shots

This is the part of the game that can really shave those strokes. It's so important to get the ball up and down when you're facing a tricky chip or a sand shot. Master this part of the game, and you can avoid those big scores that can ruin a fine round of golf...

SECRET NO. 72: EVERY SHOT IS DIFFERENT.

Every shot is different and must be analyzed to determine the best combination of options to use. The distance from the ball to the edge of the green is a factor. The distance from the edge of the green to the cup is another. The firmness of the green is a factor. The slope of the green is important to consider. What kind of trouble is present which must be avoided, such as a bunker between your ball and the green — or is there a steep drop off to a water hazard just behind the pin?

The key here is to learn how to analyze each situation and make the best possible decision.

The first and foremost decision to be made with pitches, chips and sand shots is in regard to the lie of the ball. The lie of the ball determines what you can do and can't do. It helps to determine what club you should use and how you're going to play the shot. You may want to play a pitch and run with a 5 or 6 iron, which is usually a good choice and a relatively safe play around the green. If the ball is sitting down in five inch rough, you can't play that shot. That's what I mean. The lie of the ball has eliminated that pitch and run shot from the options at your disposal.

SECRET NO. 73: CHOKE UP AND OPEN UP.

Two major keys to think about when playing your shot in most greenside situations are to choke down on the grip the closer you get to the hole and to open up your stance to play these shorter shots.

It makes sense that the less club you have below your hands, the more control you are going to have with the clubhead. Yet I see most amateurs take a standard grip on chips and short pitches. Even on the short greenside bunker escapes I choke down on the grip.

I also open up my stance on all these little finesse shots. By turning your feet and body to the left during address, you pre-determine a shorter backswing. Try it for yourself and see. Your backswing will be restricted the more you turn to the left. The shorter the shot, the more I open up. On the little bump and run shots from the fringe and other true finesse shots my feet will almost be pointing at the hole or target line, or maybe just to the right of the target line.

The average player takes way too long of a backswing in these situations, decelerates in the forward swing, hits behind it or skulls it, and his buddies tell him he looked up. Actually, from his setup position and his grip, he had very little chance of making a good shot to begin with. The shorter backswing, which the reduced shaft and the open stance will help you accomplish, is what you are after. With the shorter backswing you can make a more accelerating forward swing — more aggressive, more positive. This is the secret to many of the greenside shots.

SECRET NO. 74: RUN THE BALL WHEN YOU CAN.

Remember when I mentioned that I often carry a sand wedge with a nearly smooth face? I use it when I want to avoid adding spin to a shot. It is almost always safer and wiser to let a ball run naturally on the green. The more you spin it, the less predictable it is. If I'm in tall grass next to the green, I need a lofted club like a sand wedge to get the ball up and out of the grass as quickly as possible. But if I still have a lot of green to work with, I will probably choose this wedge. This is because I can feel confident about getting the ball clear of the heavy grass without complicating the shot by trying to figure out if and when a certain amount of spin is going to take hold. In other words, I have simplified the shot.

I think I would always recommend running the ball when it's possible. Watch the tournaments — the pros are always running the ball.

SECRET NO. 75: USE THE LEAST AMOUNT OF LOFT.

If I have a shot with a lot of green to work with, I will choose the least lofted club that will allow me to land the ball on the cut surface and not run past the hole. These are all "feel" shots so there is no way to describe them all or tell you how to play each one of them, but what you should practice in order to increase your feel for them is to choke down, open up your stance and vary the club in your hand according to the shot before you. Do not open up your clubface or close it down in these situations either. You are trying to avoid putting any side spin on the ball. That would only make it harder to control and complicate the shot unnecessarily.

Pick out a fairly flat portion of the green near the edge closest to you to land the ball. Let the loft of the club in your hand determine how far from that landing zone the ball will run. Try to use the same controlled accelerating swing and let the club choice change the overall distance.

If the shot requires the use of your sand wedge (such as a shot from deeper grass), use the flange of the club as you would in the sand. I will discuss the explosion from sand later, but this explosion from the deep grass is the same shot. If the ball is in a tight lie or on a hardpan surface, the flange of the sand wedge will work against you. This is one reason I prefer a sand wedge with not too much bounce and a fairly shallow flange. Anyway, if you must try a sand wedge shot from these riskier lies, remember to use the leading edge of the club, not the flange. Therefore, you can't open the face up on these shots, exposing the flange to the ground.

SECRET NO. 76:   IN THE SAND — OPEN THE CLUBFACE AND SWING LEFT.

First of all, sand shots from a decent lie are some of the easiest shots in golf. In most every other golf shot you play, the sweet spot of the club is supposed to contact the back of the golf ball in order to have a good result. With a sand shot, most anywhere in the sand immediately behind the ball is okay. Anyway, it really is an easy shot to get pretty good at.

As in the other greenside finesse shots, the lie, distance to the landing zone and distance from the landing to the hole must be analyzed and judged. I will begin by describing a shot from a good lie and adjust from there. One of the different factors to take in mind with this shot is the consistency and depth of the sand in the bunker.

Experience will make you better at this, but as you enter a bunker pay attention to the sand. You can feel with your feet whether it is deep or shallow. Look at it. Is it heavy grained or light and powdery? In general, the ball will come out lower and hotter if the sand is shallow, wet and/or firm and small grained. The ball will come out higher and slower if the sand is deep, loose and/or larger grained.

You want to take these factors into mind as you pick out your landing zone. You want to have a feeling of how far you will carry the ball and how far it is likely to roll after it lands. Once again, open up your stance so that your shoulder alignment is well left of the target line, and open the clubface so that the flange of the sand wedge is exposed to the surface of the sand. The flange now becomes the leading edge of the club when you do this. Ball placement should appear to be close to the right foot if viewed in relation to the target line. If viewed in relation to the line of your stance and shoulders, however, it will be in the middle or slightly forward of the middle of your stance. Remember, the object of this swing is to contact the surface of the sand behind the ball, rather than make contact with the back of the ball. If the ball is too far back in your stance, you may have a difficult time avoiding contact with the ball. I would recommend a fairly wide stance to give you better balance and to minimize the movement of the lower body in these swings. Set your weight slightly toward your left side and don't shift it much on your backswing.

Next, choke down on the grip. How much depends on the length of the shot and, in fact, is what I use to help control the distance of these shots. The closer the landing zone, the more I choke down. The swing itself is from outside the target line back down and through to the left of the target line. If you are opened up properly and you make a good outside-to-inside swing, your divot will be pointing left of the target line. In fact, it will be closer to being parallel to the line of your stance rather than the target.

For poorer lies, vary the steepness of your swing or angle of approach by getting your feet closer together and choking down on the club to the end of the grip. It is wrong to use too much body or weight shift on any of these sand shots, but as you have to swing a little harder on some of these don't be afraid to move. For the bad lies I would also suggest putting a little more weight on the left side and leaving it there throughout the swing. If the ball is buried, don't concern yourself with a follow through at all. Just let the club stick in the sand. But don't decelerate. Hit it hard.

For these escapes from bad and buried lies, count on the ball running farther than normal once they land. This will make up for some of the lack of carry you will get. These really are escapes so the main thing is to get out of the bunker and on the green ... anywhere on the green. Don't get too cute with these shots by trying to judge a landing spot right next to the edge of the bunker for a pin cut close. Accept the reality and try to make a little longer putt.

If the sand is really hard because of a recent rain and/or there wasn't much sand in the bottom of the bunker to begin with, use your pitching wedge. Because this club lacks the flange of the sand wedge, it will get down and under the ball better in these circumstances.

All of these shots are more or less explosion shots. You shouldn't be trying to pick the ball off of the top of the sand. But analyze the shot and be creative. Use your imagination. The best finesse guys are almost always the guys with a lot of imagination — Seve Ballesteros, Paul Azinger, and Tom Watson to name a few.

EVERY SHOT IS DIFFERENT

Analyze each shot to determine the best combination of options to use. The lie of the ball is the number one determinant of what you can and can't do. The distance from the ball to the edge of the green, the distance from the edge of the green to the cup, the firmness and slope of the green, and trouble spots to be avoided are all factors that need to be considered.

SECRET No. 73

CHOKE UP AND OPEN UP

Open up your stance and choke down on your grip as you get closer to the hole. The less club you have below your hands, the more control you have with the clubhead. By turning your feet and body to the left when addressing the ball, you pre-determine a shorter backswing. Open up to the point where you will actually be facing the target when you complete your swing.

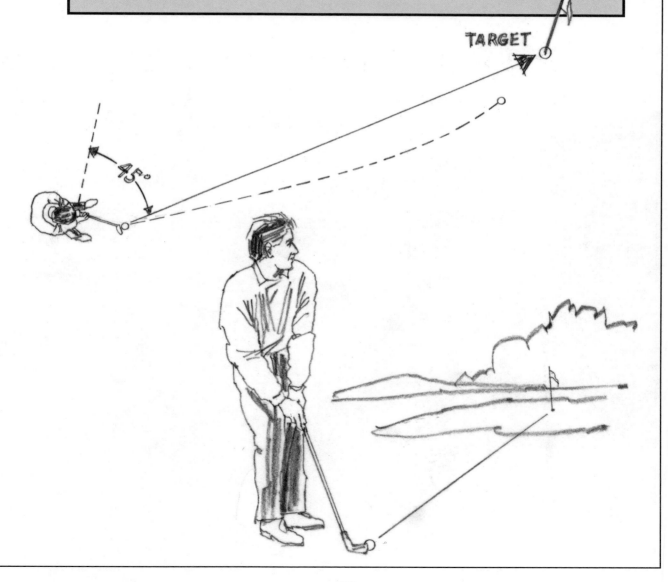

TARGET

45°

RUN THE BALL
WHEN YOU CAN

It is safer to let the ball run naturally to the hole than to try and loft a higher shot. Avoid spin on the ball because it's less predictable. In tall grass, use a sand wedge to get the ball up and out of the grass quickly. The bottom line is to simplify the shot as much as possible.

SECRET No. 75

USE THE LEAST AMOUNT OF LOFT

If you have a shot with a lot of green to work with, go with the least lofted club you have that will allow you to land the ball on the cut surface and not run past the hole. Choke down and open up your stance. Don't open or close your clubface. Pick out a flat portion of the green to land the ball, and use a controlled accelerating stroke.

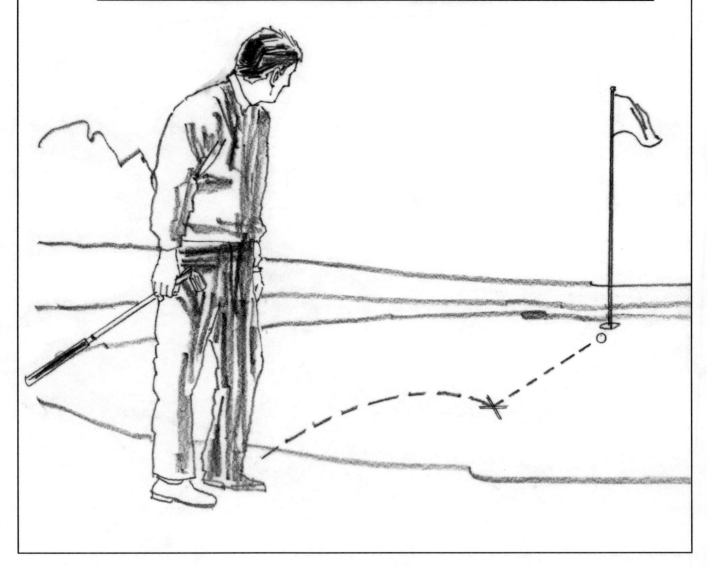

IN THE SAND — OPEN THE CLUBFACE AND SWING LEFT

Open your stance so that your shoulder alignment is well left of the target line. Set your weight slightly toward your left side. Open the clubface so that the flange is exposed to the surface of the sand. Swing from outside the target line back down and through the left of the target line. This will help compensate for the open clubface and send the ball toward the target.

TO TARGET

Part

11

The Secrets
of Putting

Y ou know what they say "You drive for show — but you putt for dough." We all know that every part of this game has to be tamed in order to seriously show up on your scorecard ... but also know that if you can't put the ball in the hole, you might as well be satisfied with playing for the pure enjoyment of the game. Let's talk about Putting ...

The subject of putting is a fascinating one and there have certainly been a number of different successful styles. Arnold Palmer made more stroke saving putts in the 60's than maybe anyone before or since. Jack Nicklaus used to stand over an important putt for so long that you wondered if he was ever going to hit it. But he sure sank a lot of them! Some of the other guys I have admired over the years are guys like George Archer and Dave Stockton. I personally learned a lot from talking and practicing with those two. Frank Beard was another good putter. And there are some on the regular tour now like Ben Crenshaw and Jay Haas who are excellent and have been so over a long time.

SECRET NO. 77: DON'T "MAKE" IT HAPPEN — "LET" IT HAPPEN.

My style or approach to putting is to let the ball find its way to the hole. I don't try to force it in there. Sometimes you read or hear people talking about hitting a short putt hard enough to take the break out of it. I prefer to make the best stroke I can and let the ball find its way in the cup. Bobby Jones putted that way too.

The way in which I try to accomplish this is to let the putter do as much of the work as possible. First, it's important in my style to be able to feel the weight of the putter-head, so I might use a little heavier putter than some people. Nothing extreme, but I want to feel the motion of the head. Next, I want to grip the club as lightly as possible so I don't cut off any of that information or "feel" that the head of the putter is sending me.

Your stance is a matter of comfort but it should accomplish a couple of important things in the process. First and most important is that your eyes should be directly above the ball. If, in your setup position, your eyes end up outside the target line of the putt, you are going to have a tough time ever getting lined up right. If your eyes are just a little inside the target line, that's not as bad. But over the ball is best. Get in your stance over a ball and without moving your head, drop another ball or something from the bridge of your nose. That will tell you where your eyes are. The other thing with your stance is that it allows a free arm swing without any appreciable body movement.

It is critical to good putting that you be relaxed and comfortable. It's hard to practice very long if you are really uncomfortable and it is really important to spend some time practicing.

11

SECRET NO. 78: USE A PENDULUM MOTION.

The stroke itself is simple enough. Most people describe it as a pendulum. That's okay as long as it doesn't make you feel the need to get mechanical with it. I like to have my palms facing out away from me a little, rather than having them face each other. This was an adjustment I made after I got on tour because it helped minimize the wrist movement in my stroke without increasing any tension in my hands. In other words, I didn't have to think about not letting my left wrist break down. I was free to think of positive things.

I do think that the speed of the back stroke and forward stroke should be as equal as possible. The length of the back stroke and forward stroke may not be equal, but the pace of the stroke should be pretty constant. Any hint of deceleration in the putting stroke will spell disaster and usually place the ball to the left of the hole. I see a lot of this among the average players.

My putting style also works best if the putter is allowed to swing freely in my hands. By this, I mean my grip pressure is so light that the putter is allowed to swing slightly back and forth by its own momentum within my grip. It is most evident when I start the back stroke because there will be just a hint of a lag between the initial movement of my hands and arms and the initial movement of the putter. Next, at the change of direction from back stroke to forward stroke, the putter will just lag behind a little bit. I'm letting the weight of the putter and in particular, the putterhead, guide the direction of the stroke.

SECRET NO. 79: GET A FEEL FOR DISTANCE.

Distance versus direction. Which is more important in putting? Well, it's hard to make many putts without solving both questions, but more 3-putts are caused by poor distance control than by bad direction. Distance putts are a matter of hand/eye coordination or "feel" and the best way to acquire it and improve upon what you've got is to practice.

Practice putts from 20 feet, 30 feet, and 40 feet, first on fairly level surfaces and then practice the same distances on moderately downhill and moderately uphill slopes. Finally, work on these distances on right to left slopes. I would work a little on left to right slopes but not too much or for any lengthy period of time. Left to right putts of any length promote an outside to inside stroke path. That's not good for you so don't dwell on these putts.

Another good drill to enhance your feel is to putt with the right hand only — the dominant one, the "feel" hand for most of us. Also, you can stroke some putts with your eyes closed. I think this is good for a couple of reasons. If you line up a putt with your eyes open and then close them, your mind does a better job of picturing the putt. It isn't

138

distracted by the ball and putter movement during the stroke. The other benefit of this drill is that because your eyes are closed, you will become less ball bound, less conscious of the moment of impact. I've cautioned against anticipating the hit in other parts of the book, but the smaller the stroke, the more important it becomes. On a putt or a finesse shot around the green, we are swinging with less effort, and therefore we have a tendency to over-control the club with our hands. Anticipating the moment of impact almost always causes deceleration. In the small strokes, that will usually mean a poor result.

SECRET NO. 80: "DRILL" THE SHORT ONES.

For short putts of two or three feet, (which, by the way, is what I spend the majority of my putting practice time working on), I really like one drill in particular. Lay two long irons down on the green with their grip ends at either side of the hole and parallel to each other. Turn your toes to the outside and try to do this on a flat portion of your practice green.

Start with the ball about a foot from the hole, line up a putt and stroke it in using your best setup position and stroke. The parallel irons will help you see whether or not your blade is square to the hole or not. You can't miss very easily because the ball is in between the clubs. What you want to do is feed your subconscious mind with the picture of a perfectly square putterface and of the ball going into the cup ... every time. When you are making solid one foot putts, move back and work on two footers and finally on three footers from inside the two irons.

Notice that the stroke necessary to make the one foot putt is the same as for the two foot putt. On fast greens, it's the same as for three foot putts. Build your confidence and when you face a three footer for all the marbles on the course, you'll be able to give it your one footer stroke and in she'll go.

SECRET NO. 81: READ THE GREEN.

I like to think of the slope and contour of a green the way water would flow if it were poured on the surface. Lots of putts are a little downhill and a little sidehill at the same time. Just visualize the way water would flow.

Start looking at the overall position of the green as you approach it. If you're riding in a cart it's a little harder to do. When you play your approach shot to the green, take your putter with you and walk the last 100 yards or so to the green. If you're in the southern part of the country where Bermuda greens are predominant, figure out which way west is and/or if there is a nearby lake or river where the runners common to Bermuda are going to grow. Is the course subject to an area wide slope from a nearby

mountain range? As you get closer you can begin to get a feeling about the portion of the green where the hole and your ball are. I like to read putts from the lowest side or end of the line. But it doesn't hurt to get a look at it from more than one perspective. The faster the surface of a green, the more a sloping putt will break. You will have to allow for that.

SECRET NO. 82: BREAK IT DOWN.

When I'm reading a sloping putt of any length, I like to break the putt down into smaller parts. If that first sounds like a complication, stay with me, it's really another way to simplify.

On a three footer, for instance, if it breaks say two inches I like to imagine the line it will actually take from the center of the cup back to the ball and find a spot a few inches in front of my ball along that line. Then I line up the blade on that spot, make my one foot putting stroke and what could be simpler than that. I've reduced the three footer to a four incher and given it the most practiced and familiar putting stroke I've got.

I do that same process for longer breaking putts except I may have more than one spot or target for longer distances. It also depends on how much break I anticipate. I don't think I've ever used more than three spots for any length putt.

I have a good imagination. If you do too, try to "see" a depression or trough in the green between the cup and your ball. Sometimes I do this on straight putts and I swear it's like there's no way to keep it out of the hole. It just can't get out of that trough.

SECRET NO. 83: FIND THE "REAL" CENTER OF THE CUP.

One more word about breaking putts which is really important for you to understand. On a breaking putt, the center of the cup is not the portion of the cup nearest your ball. The center is actually toward the uphill side of the cup. In other words, as a ball breaks down the slope, it's the side of the cup to some degree or another, which then becomes the side of the hole facing the ball. Hope that's not too confusing. The importance of this is that if you're judging distance and the line, don't use the lip of the cup nearest your ball to aim. In fact, on a severely breaking putt, the front of the cup becomes the side of the hole in relation to the line.

SECRET No. 77

DON'T "MAKE" IT HAPPEN — "LET" IT HAPPEN

My style of putting is to let the ball find its own way to the hole. Don't try to force it in there. I do this by using a little heavier putter and letting it do as much of the work as possible. Get a comfortable stance with your eyes directly over the ball, and be sure you allow a free arm swing without any appreciable body movement.

SECRET No. 78

USE A PENDULUM MOTION

A good way to think about your putting stroke is to imagine it as a pendulum — as long as it doesn't make you feel the need to get too mechanical with it. The speed of the back stroke and forward stroke should be as equal as possible — the length of each doesn't necessarily have to be equal. Finally, be sure that you accelerate through the ball. Any hint of deceleration could spell disaster.

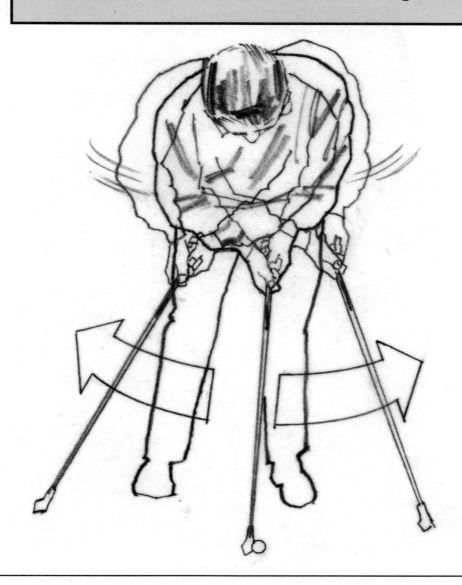

GET A FEEL FOR DISTANCE

More 3-putts are caused by poor distance control than by bad direction. Distance putts are a matter of hand/eye coordination or "feel" — that can only be acquired through practice. Practice putts from 20, 30, and 40 feet, first on flat, and then sloping surfaces. Also, try stroking some putts with your eyes closed to get a better mental picture, and become less "ball bound."

SECRET No. 80

"DRILL" THE SHORT ONES

A practice drill I like to use in particular for short putts is to lay down two irons in a path on either side of the hole and parallel to each other. Start with one footers, then move back to two and three footers. The irons will help you square your blade to the hole, and will feed your subconscious mind with the picture of a perfectly square putterface sending the ball into the cup ... every time.

READ THE GREEN

Start to read the green by looking at the overall position of the green as you approach it. As you get closer, you can begin to get a feeling about the portion of the green where the hole and your ball is. I like to visualize the slope and contour of a green as the way water would flow if it were poured on its surface. It doesn't hurt to get a look at your putt from more than one perspective.

SECRET No. 82

BREAK IT DOWN

I like to break a putt of any length down into smaller parts. For instance, on a three footer, imagine the line it will take from the center of the cup back to the ball and pick a spot just a few inches in front of your ball along that line. Then, simply hit over that spot. You've just reduced a three foot putt to a four-incher. Use the same process for longer breaking putts.

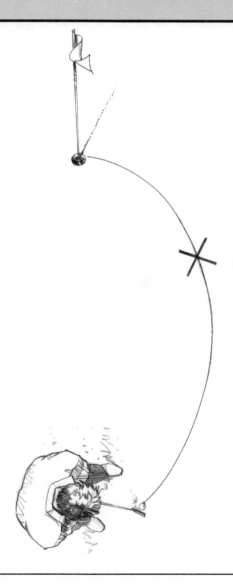

FIND THE "REAL" CENTER
OF THE CUP

Get a feel for where the "true" center of the cup is while putting. Most amateurs just figure that the center is simply the part of the hole nearest your ball at address. This can be misleading for severely sloping putts. The center of the hole is actually the part that the ball will be facing as it curls in from the high side.

Part

12

The Secrets of Overcoming Impairments of Age & Other Physical Handicaps

12

I've had to make a number of adjustments in my game over the last decade and a half. And I have an idea of what adjusting to new circumstances is all about.

Some of it I've learned through trial and error and some through talking with other players, especially those now on the Senior PGA Tour.

When lightning injured my back in the mid-70's, I hoped those lower back pains would eventually go away. They didn't, and I've had a recurrent back problem ever since.

So whether from injury or the natural effect of the aging process, we are forced into making a few changes in our game. So what? It's still the greatest sport in the world and truly a sport for a lifetime.

SECRET NO. 84: UNDERSTAND YOUR LIMITATIONS.

As a senior golfer, you are probably facing some limitations that you never even thought about a few short years ago. Even if you are healthy, and I hope you are, you could still be losing distance. The natural aging process diminishes our suppleness and flexibility. Unless or until medical science figures out a way to counter this process, we are going to have to face our new limitations.

You may not want to hear this, but if the golf course or courses you play regularly seem to be getting longer and golf is becoming less enjoyable to you because you can't reach any greens in regulation anymore ... move up. I know a lot of courses that I visit throughout southwestern Florida have slightly shorter tee boxes set aside for senior players. It will only frustrate you and begin to create bad habits in your swing if you are straining to get every last yard out of every shot.

If you're having to hit two fairway woods after your tee shot on a lot of par 5 holes, you're playing too much golf course. Where you used to use a 6 or 7 iron to approach a particular green, you're now faced with a 3 or 4 iron. And I'll bet the lower shot that you get from that longer iron won't stop very well, so you either have to land it perfectly on the front edge or you're going to be facing a chip back to the putting surface. That's not right. Just as life is rewarding you for all those years of hard work and you're at a point when you can play the game you love so much, about as often as you want, it's becoming more frustration than fun.

I'm going to make some other suggestions and tell you what some of my older friends on the Senior PGA Tour are doing to overcome the aging process, but the first one is face reality. You know the senior pros are playing much shorter courses than the regular tour. Play a course that can be enjoyable to you. Get back to playing some short irons into those greens by moving to the forward tees on your course.

12

SECRET NO. 85: TRIM DOWN AND LOOSEN UP.

If you hated what I told you in the last secret, you're really going to love me now. Lose weight! Get out and walk! Seriously, I can't prescribe a diet for you or recommend an exercise program. I'm not a doctor, I'm a golf pro. I can tell you this, though: most of my friends from about 40 on up through the guys already on the Senior Tour have gotten themselves into a regular program of stretching and aerobic training. They do it because it works. You've heard the saying "Use it or lose it!" Well, I don't know if that applies to everything, but when it comes to strength and flexibility, I certainly think it's true.

In a few short years, I'm going to be ready for the Senior Tour and I want to be as ready and as good as I can be. I'm looking forward to the competition, to seeing and playing golf with all my old friends again. I really want to pick their pockets when I get there. So, I want to be at my best.

Consult your doctor before starting an exercise program. As the commercial says, "Just Do It!" I would say that any good aerobic exercise that you choose, whether it be jogging, walking, swimming, hiking or stair climbing in the gym or at the "Y", will do the most good for you. Aerobic exercise, by its very nature, gets the blood going good to all parts of the body and I really believe it helps both your physical fitness and your mental and emotional fitness as well. It gives me a general feeling of well being and confidence and these are great things to have going for you when it comes to golf, regardless of your age.

Also, you know how you feel when you over eat or have been eating the wrong foods. Eat hearty, but eat healthy. Your whole body will reward you. Besides losing an inch or two, it will give you just the excuse you need to buy a new golf outfit or two.

I really feel sorry for non-golfers sometimes because golfers have so much fun. We get to wear the best looking clothes. We get to enjoy some unbelievable works of landscape art. We get to experience the outdoors with all its wildlife and beauty. We get to tell stories with each other and laugh. We get to compete at the most gentile of sports. And when we're through, we go to the clubhouse or grill room, tell more stories , laugh a little more, share a cold beverage with one another and make a plan to do it all over again! Golf is so much fun, it's just not fair to the other sports.

Stretching is the last element in this secret and is so overlooked by many golfers. More than strength, flexibility is your ticket to more distance on the golf course. Remembering the Ball Flight Laws from Part 5, clubhead speed is the primary influence on distance. Fast flexible muscles make the club go faster, not large bulky muscles.

I do think that as you get older, you need to begin to do *some* strength training if you haven't been very physical or athletic throughout your life. Women often need to work a little more on strength in order to maintain control of the club. But if you have always been a fairly strong person, work on flexibility. It's much more valuable to you.

As you know, both the regular and the Senior PGA Tours have traveling health centers now where the players can go to get a good, safe workout. My friend Bruce

Crampton uses it regularly, as do Gary Player, Dale Douglass, and many others.

SECRET NO. 86: SENIOR EQUIPMENT.

Throughout the golf industry right now, we are experiencing a tremendous boom in the development of new equipment. Companies and people all over the world are spending a lot of dollars creating new and better clubs, balls, training aids, etc. There has never been a technology explosion in our sport like the one with us now.

As Director of Golf at South Seas Plantation, this means a lot of hard work just to stay abreast of everything coming out. But it is so interesting, it is really a labor of love.

For the first time, golf club manufacturers have started designing clubs specifically for seniors. These clubs are usually about a half inch longer than their regular models, graphite shafted and either metal or graphite headed. Whole sets are created with the senior player in mind.

The senior clubs are made the way they are to (1) try and increase your clubhead speed, and (2) get the ball airborne a little faster. They really work, too. The graphite shafts and/or heads are lighter. Now, with no more effort and possibly a little less, you will be swinging a longer club which translates into greater clubhead speed.

On top of that, most of the manufacturers have moved the "kick" or flex point down the shaft toward the clubhead. This lower kick point gets the ball up in the air faster and makes the trajectory of the shot somewhat higher. This will help you on your approach shots. When you switch to these clubs, you will regain some of your lost distance and some of the playability you used to have in your traditional set.

SECRET NO. 87: WORK ON YOUR SHORT GAME.

It's funny how people think about things sometimes. Like when you get older and lose some distance off your tee to green game, people assume you're going to be a great chipper and putter. Well, if your short game was weak before, you can bet it hasn't gotten better just because you got older.

The thing is, you will probably never get your full distance back, but if you work on your short game, it is possible it could improve. If you relied on distance in your game and you've had an injury that has cost you some yards, the only place left for you to turn is your short game. Here again, you might want to consider some equipment changes.

A third wedge is probably of more use to you than a 2 iron. You might also want to consider the long shafted putters. They've proven themselves in the senior circuit over the past several years. They work for you in two ways. They eliminate the wrist hinge

12

which is the potential trouble spot in any putting stroke. If it steadies out guys like my buddy Orville Moody, it really works. The second benefit from the longer putters is the reduced strain on your back. There are no two ways about it, putting practice is hard on the back at any age. The long putters really help. You'll need to work with one for a while until you learn the technique, but once you get used to it, they can be a real weapon for you.

If you're wearing bifocals or trifocals, think about getting some sport glasses; the kind with reading correction in the corner or top of the glasses, or at least get the "duo-line" graduated kind. You need good eye sight, and in particular, depth perception, to have a good short game. Refer to the chapters pertaining to chipping, sand play and putting for the techniques that will strengthen this more-important-than-ever part of your game.

SECRET NO. 88: RIDE THE CLUB.

Finally, in this chapter, let me tell you what I've learned about adjusting to having a bad or occasionally bad back. The swing I grew up making and the one that carried me through four out of my five PGA Tour victories was a hard turn and clearing of the left side. My head stayed solidly behind the ball through impact. This is the way to hit a golf ball, if you can.

Now I can't, at least not very often. When I won my last tour event, the Atlanta Golf Classic, I did it with a swing designed to take some of the pressure off of my back. I rode the club through the hitting area instead of staying behind it. It has actually become rather popular with some of today's best known teachers. The head and upper body move more laterally and you finish in an upright position, ahead of the ball position, facing the target. The difference between this swing and the more traditional move is in allowing the head to move laterally, both in the backswing, just a little and in the follow through, quite a bit. The danger is in allowing the head to move up and down. Don't let it "bob," but give it some freedom.

Another thing you can do to get a little more freedom in your turn is to flare the toes of your feet out a little more than normal. Maybe thirty degrees or so in each direction. With the right foot pointed right of perpendicular to the target line, your backswing can get a little longer. Also, be sure to allow your left heel to come off the ground more than you used to. A slightly narrower stance will promote more hip turn than you've had. By having your left foot turned out a little, you'll be able to get through the ball better, your left hip will clear sooner and your balance will be improved. Find the stance that allows you the most freedom to turn in both directions.

The basics of alignment and swing still hold true for you, but you must make some of these compromises for flexibility, balance and movement to continue to get the most out of your game.

UNDERSTAND
YOUR LIMITATIONS

Understand the frustrations that could become part of your game if you don't consider playing courses that are shorter, and more open to "iron" play. Or, get back to playing some short irons into those greens by moving up to the shorter tees on your course.

SECRET No. 85

TRIM DOWN AND LOOSEN UP

Number one ... lose weight! And number two ... exercise! Any good aerobic program that you choose, whether it be jogging, walking, swimming, hiking, stair climbing, or working out at the "Y" will do you the most good. Eat hearty, but eat healthy. And stretching is *so* important. Flexibility is your ticket to more distance on the golf course.

SENIOR EQUIPMENT

For the first time, golf manufacturers have started designing clubs exclusively for seniors. They are usually a little longer than their regular models, graphite shafted, with either a metal or graphite head. Basically, what they do is help you (1) increase your clubhead speed, and (2) get the ball airborne a little faster.

SECRET No. 87

WORK ON YOUR SHORT GAME

As you get older, you will probably never get your full distance back, but if you work on your short game it is possible that it could improve your score. A third wedge is probably more useful to you than a 2 iron. Also consider the long-shafted putters. They eliminate the wrist hinge that could become more of a factor with age, and they reduce a lot of strain on your back.

"RIDE THE CLUB"

When I won my last tour event, the Atlanta Golf Classic, I did it with a swing designed to take some of the pressure off my back. Instead of keeping my head solidly behind the ball through impact, I "rode" the club through the hitting area — allowing my head to move laterally, both in the backswing and in the follow through.

Part

13

Secret
Practice Drills
of the
Big-Money Pros

When it comes to practice drills in golf, there really aren't many "secrets" because everybody knows about — and practices — the ones that really work. Here are a few of the best on the following pages that I and other pros use to keep on top of our game. They should help yours too . . .

13

SECRET DRILL No. 1

MOTEL DRILL

PURPOSE: Swing plane grooving

DESCRIPTION: Standing at the foot of and between two beds arranged like most motel rooms, swing club back and forth, ticking the bed, going back, coming down, and going back up. Start in slow motion and add speed. Soft pillows on chairs may be substituted for beds.

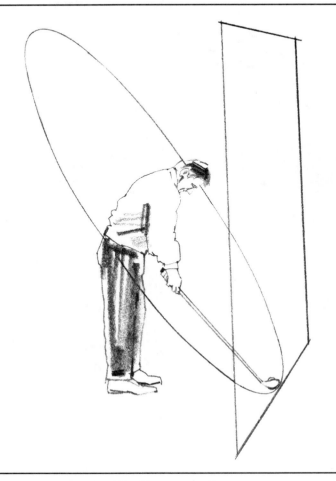

SECRET DRILL No. 2

THE CIRCLE AND THE PLANE

PURPOSE: Swing plane grooving

DESCRIPTION: Take your normal stance and address position. Imagine a horizontal wall — or plane — parallel to your stance, planted right at the clubhead. As you swing, imagine you're making a complete circle that intersects at the point of contact with the ball at the base of the plane.

13

SECRET DRILL No. 3

SHOE BOX

PURPOSE: Inside to inside clubhead path

DESCRIPTION: Put shoe box or comparable object just outside target line so toe of club is within 1/2". Practice hitting shots. If box is contacted before ball, swing path is outside/in. If box is contacted after ball, swing path is inside/out. If club does not contact box, swing path is inside/inside, which is correct for standard shots.

SECRET DRILL No. 4

LEFT ARM ONLY

PURPOSE: Left side control and correction

DESCRIPTION: Make normal left hand grip with short iron, ball on tee to begin. Hold left elbow with right hand. Turn and make good left arm only swings, being sure to turn body back and through.

13

SECRET DRILL No. 5

RIGHT ARM ONLY

PURPOSE: Right side control and correction

DESCRIPTION: Make normal right hand grip with short iron, ball on tee to begin. Hold right elbow with left hand. Turn and make good right arm only swings, being sure to turn body back and through.

SECRET DRILL No. 6

BASEBALL STRIDE

PURPOSE: Improve weight shift

DESCRIPTION: Take normal stance, ball on tee, use short or mid iron. Start backswing and move left foot next to right. At start of downswing, move left foot back to original position and swing through.

13

SECRET DRILL No. 7

HORIZONTAL PLANE

PURPOSE: Build swing speed

DESCRIPTION: Take stance but hold driver out from shoulders, parallel to ground. Swing as hard as possible in horizontal plane then tilt plane and swing with same speed. Continue tilting plane until you are brushing top of grass or clipping tee out of ground.

SECRET DRILL No. 8

"T" DRILL FOR PRACTICE RANGE

PURPOSE: Alignment and ball position

DESCRIPTION: Variation on laying clubs on the ground, draw "T" on ground with biodegradable marking paint. One line is target line and other is ball position. Better than with clubs because you can't put a club exactly on target line and you may be cautious of stepping on ball position club.

13

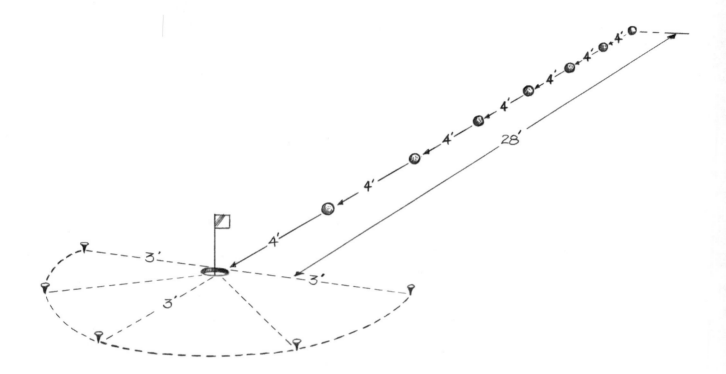

SECRET DRILL No. 9

BALL DRILL

PURPOSE: Improve distance control

DESCRIPTION: Put half circle of tees 3 feet even with and behind hole. Place balls 4 feet apart in straight line on level putting surface. Practice putting balls, starting with closest and moving out. Putts must reach hole but not go beyond tees. Must start drill over if a ball is short of cup or runs outside of half circle.

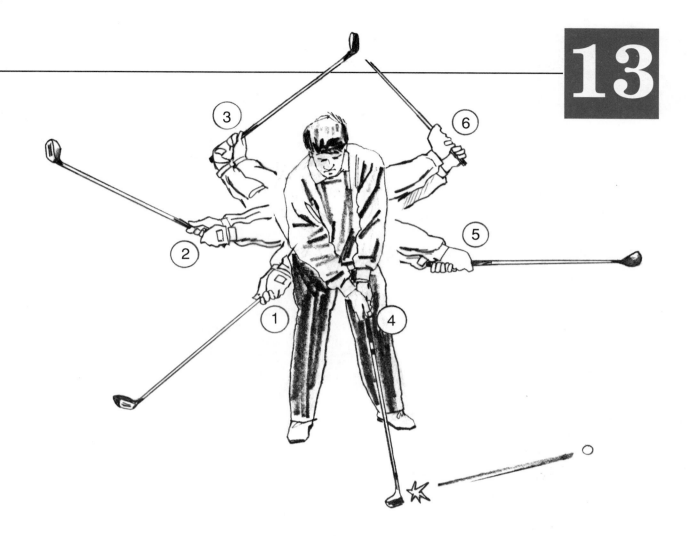

SECRET DRILL No. 10

BY THE NUMBERS

PURPOSE: Tempo improvement

DESCRIPTION: Count out loud on practice tee while hitting balls. 1, 2, 3 on the back swing and 4, 5, 6 on forward swing. Voice should remain steady and pace of numbers should be evenly spaced. Watch out for too much intensity on "4."

13

SECRET DRILL No. 11

IN THE DARK

PURPOSE: Improve feel and visualization

DESCRIPTION: On practice chipping green and putting green, line up long putts and chip shots with eyes open. Close eyes and make stroke/swing. "See" the shot with your mind.

SECRET DRILL No. 12

SEEK YOUR OWN PATH

PURPOSE: Increase arc and swing freedom

DESCRIPTION: Swing 2 or 3 clubs or a weighted club and let club seek its own path. Let club swing you by relaxing arms and hands.

The Basic
Swing Checklist
of the
Big-Money Pros

What follows is a very detailed list of the in-swing body positions common to the basic swing. I chose the driver for this sequence, but except for the width of the stance, the swing mechanics will be the same for all clubs.

Two views of the swing are portrayed on each page, followed by a description of the ideal position and/or movement for ten key elements of the body. On each page you will be able to follow the continuous motion of each part of the swing in which you are interested. You can study the position of all body parts at any given moment of the swing or follow one swing element throughout the swing. Pay attention to the direction and timing of each element, as well as the positions.

1 AT ADDRESS

1	**FEET:**	Standard width, weight even, left foot toed out 15 °, balance ball/heel.
2	**KNEES:**	Slightly flexed.
3	**HIPS:**	Square to slightly open.
4	**SHOULDERS:**	Square to slightly open, left somewhat higher than right.
5	**ARMS:**	Hanging freely, left extended, right flexed slightly.
6	**WRISTS:**	Relaxed and facing one another, thumbs on top of grip.
7	**CLUB:**	Face square, shaft perpendicular to target line, 2 inches inside left heel.
8	**SPINE ANGLE:**	Inclined about 25 ° from vertical.
9	**CENTER:**	Slightly behind ball for short clubs, more for longer.
10	**HEAD:**	Chin up, eyes focused on ball.

11	**FEET:**	Weight evenly distributed.
12	**KNEES:**	Right flexed and still, left flexed, starting to move right.
13	**HIPS:**	Left hip turning toward right, right barely moving.
14	**SHOULDERS:**	Turning right on nearly level plane.
15	**ARMS:**	Left extended and parallel to target line, right folded.
16	**WRISTS:**	Just beginning to cock, thumbs on top of grip.
17	**CLUB:**	Club parallel to target line, toe vertical.
18	**SPINE ANGLE:**	Constant.
19	**CENTER:**	Moving right with swing.
20	**HEAD:**	Slight lateral movement to right.

21	**FEET:**	Weight toward heels and inside right foot, left heel lifting.
22	**KNEES:**	Right flexed still, left planted right behind ball.
23	**HIPS:**	Left has moved right, right has completed turn (45°).
24	**SHOULDERS:**	Still relatively level near complete 90° turn.
25	**ARMS:**	Left extended, right folded and underneath club.
26	**WRISTS:**	Cocked almost 90°, thumbs under grip.
27	**CLUB:**	Head on plane, butt pointing at target line.
28	**SPINE ANGLE:**	Constant.
29	**CENTER:**	Behind ball.
30	**HEAD:**	Steady in slightly lateral position.

TOP OF BACK SWING

4

31	**FEET:**	Left heel replants, weight starting left.
32	**KNEES:**	Right flexed and still, left starts moving left.
33	**HIPS:**	Full turn 45 °.
34	**SHOULDERS:**	Full turn 90 °.
35	**ARMS:**	Left extended, right forearm 90 ° to shaft.
36	**WRISTS:**	Fully cocked, thumbs under grip, left parallel to clubface.
37	**CLUB:**	Near parallel to ground and parallel to target line.
38	**SPINE ANGLE:**	Constant.
39	**CENTER:**	Steady behind ball.
40	**HEAD:**	Steady behind ball.

41	**FEET:**	Weight moving left, right heel still down flat.
42	**KNEES:**	Right shifts toward target, left turning left slightly.
43	**HIPS:**	Turning left and moving laterally toward target.
44	**SHOULDERS:**	Left turning left, right moving down.
45	**ARMS:**	Pulled down by rotation of lower body.
46	**WRISTS:**	Still fully cocked, left flat and parallel to clubface.
47	**CLUB:**	On or just under plane, butt pointing at target line.
48	**SPINE ANGLE:**	Constant.
49	**CENTER:**	Slightly moving left, but still behind ball.
50	**HEAD:**	Steady.

51	**FEET:**	Weight moving left, right heel still down flat.
52	**KNEES:**	Rotating left, right pointing toward ball.
53	**HIPS:**	Turning left and open to target line.
54	**SHOULDERS:**	Turning left behind lower body.
55	**ARMS:**	Right elbow close to body, left extended downward.
56	**WRISTS:**	Beginning to uncock, left flat and parallel to clubface, thumbs on top of grip.
57	**CLUB:**	Lagging behind hands, toe vertical.
58	**SPINE ANGLE:**	Constant.
59	**CENTER:**	Just behind ball.
60	**HEAD:**	Steady.

7

61	**FEET:**	Weight moving left, right heel being pulled up.
62	**KNEES:**	Left straightening, right at ball.
63	**HIPS:**	Opening to target line.
64	**SHOULDERS:**	Left shoulder higher and turning left.
65	**ARMS:**	Left extended, right straightening slightly.
66	**WRISTS:**	Left facing target, releasing.
67	**CLUB:**	Clubface square to target.
68	**SPINE ANGLE:**	Constant.
69	**CENTER:**	Slightly behind ball.
70	**HEAD:**	Steady.

71	**FEET:**	Weight to outside left heel, right heel pulled up.
72	**KNEES:**	Right even with left, left straight but not locked.
73	**HIPS:**	Open almost 90 ° to target line.
74	**SHOULDERS:**	Open almost 90 ° to target line.
75	**ARMS:**	Right extended, left elbow folding close to body.
76	**WRISTS:**	Left flat and parallel to face, thumbs on top of grip.
77	**CLUB:**	Parallel to target line, toe vertical.
78	**SPINE ANGLE:**	Constant.
79	**CENTER:**	Over left heel.
80	**HEAD:**	Moving left slightly.

9 FULL FOLLOW THROUGH

81	**FEET:**	Weight to outside, left heel balanced.
82	**KNEES:**	Even, with left supporting weight.
83	**HIPS:**	Right closer to target than left.
84	**SHOULDERS:**	Open over 90 °, slightly behind hip line.
85	**ARMS:**	Folded to absorb momentum of swing.
86	**WRISTS:**	Cocked, thumbs under grip.
87	**CLUB:**	Full finish behind back.
88	**SPINE ANGLE:**	Nearly upright.
89	**CENTER:**	Over left foot.
90	**HEAD:**	Up and facing target over left foot.

THE COMPLETE GOLF SWING

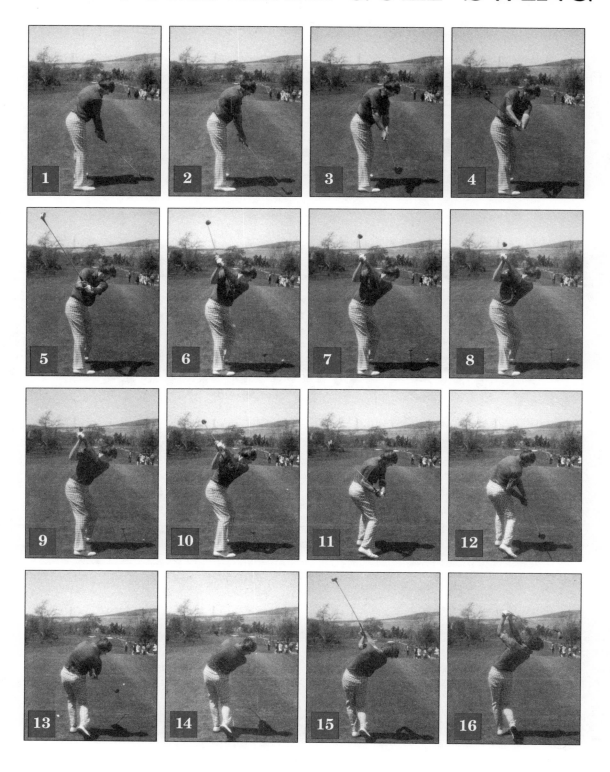

Situation Checklist
of the
Big-Money Pros

Gary Player has always likened golf tournaments to examinations. Certainly the major competitions like the British Open and the U. S. Open test us in every facet of the game. Now I'm not the academic type, and I don't care too much for tests or examinations. No sense making life any more difficult than it has to be.

What follows is my "Situation Checklist of the Big-Money Pros". It presents most of the routine as well as many of the unusual circumstances in which golfers find themselves. For each situation or condition it recommends a solution in the form of a checklist of various ways to approach the shot. This type of presentation cannot be totally comprehensive because every shot you play is just a little different from every other one. The strength of the wind will vary, and the degree to which you want to fade or draw a shot will depend on all the factors affecting a shot. You must make these decisions on the course for yourself.

This reference is a place to start and a place to learn. Practice the alignment adjustments on the range and become comfortable with them before attempting them on the course. Learn for yourself how much you need to open or close a clubface to change the flight of the ball, etc.

It is necessary to assume that your normal shot is a straight ball. As I mentioned earlier, Johnny Miller is the only tour player I can remember who consistently hit the ball straight. Use the straight ball assumption as a point of reference. For example, if your normal ball flight is a fade (left to right) and the Situation Checklist recommends opening the clubface, opening your stance, etc. in order to fade the ball, don't. You already do this naturally. Just play your normal shot. On the other hand, if you normally fade the ball and the shot calls for a draw (right to left) you will probably have to make more of an adjustment than the "slightly" open alignment recommended by the checklist. In other words, you will need to personalize the chart. And I would recommend you make notes on it as you learn to use it more effectively.

As you already know, one of the key elements to playing good golf is to play the percentage shot. I believe in that. Whenever possible play your natural, no adjustment shot. Don't be trying to work the ball all over the golf course for every shot you face. Keep the game simple. Listen to Jerry.

Early in his career Jack Nicklaus overpowered golf courses and his competition. His strength was his length. Later on he became an even better player because he learned how to think his way around the golf course. He made better risk/reward decisions than anyone else. When you decide to play a shot other than your normal shot on the golf course, weigh the risk/reward consequences first. You may decide that playing a familiar shot a little closer to the hazard is better than trying an unfamiliar shot that could lead to disaster.

SITUATION	Club Selection					Grip					Stance			Body Alignment				
	Normal	+1	+2	-1	-2	Neutral	Stronger	Weaker	Firmer	Lighter	Normal	Wider	Narrower	Square	Slightly open	Slightly closed	Very open	Very closed
Drive, down wind	•					•					•			•				
Drive, up wind	•						•					•					•	
Drive, right to left wind	•						•			•	•					•		
Drive, left to right wind	•							•	•		•				•			
Drive, maximum distance	•					•			•		•			•				
Approach, down wind				•	•	•			•		•			•				
Approach, up wind		•	•			•						•					•	
Approach, right to left wind		•						•	•		•				•			
Approach, left to right wind				•			•			•	•						•	
Approach to elevated green		•				•					•			•				
Approach to depressed green				•		•					•			•				
Approach to hard green	•					•							•		•			
Approach to soft green		•				•			•		•			•				
Approach to undulating green		•				•		•			•					•		
Escape from fwy bunker - good lie		•				•						•			•			
Escape from fwy bunker - bad lie					•		•					•					•	
Escape from pine straw		•				•						•		•				
Escape from dead leaves		•				•						•		•				
Escape from hardpan	•					•					•			•				
Escape from muddy ground		•				•						•		•				
Escape from light rough				•		•					•			•				
Escape from deep rough				•		•		•					•		•			
Escape from trees (low)			•				•					•					•	
Escape from trees (high)				•		•							•		•			
Escape from water hazards				•		•		•				•					•	
Escape from grnsd bunker - good lie	•					•						•					•	
Escape from grnsd bunker - bad lie	•					•		•					•				•	
Escape from grnsd bunker - buried lie	•					•		•					•		•			
Shot from uphill lie		•	•			•							•				•	
Shot from downhill lie				•	•	•						•			•			
Shot from sloping lie - away		•				•					•				•			
Shot from sloping lie - toward	•					•					•						•	
Pitch shot - normal	•					•				•			•		•			
Pitch shot - no spin	•					•		•	•				•		•			
Punch shot	•					•			•				•		•			
Knockdown shot		•				•						•				•		
Lob shot	•							•		•			•				•	
Chip shot	•					•							•				•	
Extreme left to right shot			•					•	•			•					•	
Extreme right to left shot					•		•			•	•							•

Clubface Alignment					Ball Position				Swing Plane					Swing Length				Visualization
Square	Slightly open	Slightly closed	Very open	Very closed	Normal	1" forward	1" back	2+" back	Inside/inside	Inside/out	Outside/in	Shallow	Steep	Full	3/4	1/2	Less	
●						●			●					●				Higher shot
		●					●		●					●				Lower shot
		●					●			●				●				Ride the wind
	●					●			●					●				Ride the wind
●					●				●					●				Zero tension
●							●		●					●				Club down
		●					●		●						●			Boring flight
	●					●			●					●				Up against for control
		●					●			●				●				Up against for control
●					●				●					●				Add club
●					●				●					●				Subtract club
	●				●				●					●				Slight cut shot
●					●				●					●				Hit and stick
	●				●				●					●				Add club/cut shot
	●						●		●		●				●			Controlled fade
			●				●				●	●		●				Get out in one
●					●				●		●				●			Good balance pick it
●					●				●		●				●			Under control
●							●		●					●				Catch it clean
●					●				●						●			Aim safely
●					●				●					●				Beware of flyer
	●						●				●	●		●				Clubface will close
		●					●			●					●			More club/less effort
	●					●					●	●		●				Make sure you get out
			●			●					●			●				Explosion shot
			●			●					●					●	●	Choke down
			●			●					●		●		●			Ball will roll
●						●			●				●	●				Stay down/get out
●						●			●		●			●				Beware of pull
●							●		●		●			●				Beware of push
		●			●				●					●				Ball will curve right
	●				●				●					●				Ball will curve left
	●							●	●						●	●	●	Choke down/hit firm
	●						●			●					●	●	●	Long slow swing
	●						●			●	●			●				Block your release
		●					●			●	●			●				Release hands
			●			●					●		●	●		●	●	Soft touch
		●						●	●		●					●	●	Get it rolling fast
			●			●					●			●				Block it out
				●			●			●				●				Fast hands